The
NATIONAL PARKS
and Other Wild Places of
THE
PHILIPPINES

The
NATIONAL PARKS
and Other Wild Places of
THE
PHILIPPINES

Nigel Hicks

NH
NEW
HOLLAND

First published in 2000 by New Holland Publishers (UK) Ltd
London • Cape Town • Sydney • Auckland

2 4 6 8 10 9 7 5 3 1

24 Nutford Place, London W1H 6DQ, United Kingdom

80 McKenzie Street, Cape Town 8001, South Africa

Level 1/Unit 4, 14 Aquatic Drive, Frenchs Forest, NSW 2086, Australia

218 Lake Road, Northcote, Auckland, New Zealand

ISBN 1 85974 194 0

Project Manager: Jo Hemmings
Series Editor: Mike Unwin
Copy Editor: Nigel Collar
Designer: Behram Kapadia
Cover Design: Alan Marshall
Cartography: William Smuts
Index: Blueline Editorial Services
Production: Joan Woodroffe

Reproduction by Pica Colour Separation Overseas (Pte) Ltd, Singapore
Printed and bound in Singapore by Star Standard Industries (Pte) Ltd

Publishers' Note

Throughout this book species are, where possible, referred to by their common as opposed to scientific
names for ease of reference by the general reader. Where no common names exist, scientific names are
used. Many of the titles listed in the further reading section on page 172 provide full scientific names for
species found in The Philippines. The maps contained in the book are intended as 'locators' only; detailed,
large-scale maps should be consulted when planning a trip. It is important to note that access, accommodation and other details vary as new transport methods and facilities develop. Remember that trail routes can
vary, river courses can change, and water depths can alter dramatically within minutes. Although the publishers, author and consultants have made every effort to ensure that the information contained in this book
was correct at the time of going to press, they accept no responsibility for any loss, injury or inconvenience
sustained by any person using the book.

Map legend for section maps
shown between pages 22 and 166

Symbol	Description	Symbol	Description
▦▦▦▦▦	Motorway	Cabugao ⊚	Village or small town
———	Main road	Park HQ ▣	General information
———	Secondary road	Palogtok Falls ●	Place of interest
- - - - -	Track	Agusan	Water feature
MALAYSIA	International boundary	Mt Bulusan 1559m ▲ (5115ft)	Peak in metres (feet)
- - - - - -	Protected Area boundary	✈	International airport
Manila ⊚	City or major town	✦	Domestic airport

Illustrations appearing in the preliminary pages are as follows:
Half title: Philippine Tarsier; Title pages: Mangroves and coconut palms on Siargao
Island, Mindanao; Pages 4–5: Offshore rocks at low tide, Batanes Islands; Pages 6–7:
The Cordillera Central, northern Luzon; Pages 8–9: Sunset on Calauit Island Wildlife
Sanctuary, Palawan.

CONTENTS

FOREWORD

The Philippine Tourism Master Plan, the blueprint for tourism development until the year 2010, commissioned by the Department of Tourism in cooperation with the World Tourism Organization and the United Nations Development Programme, was completed in 1991. Among its objectives was to develop tourism on an environmentally sustainable basis. This placed the Philippine Department of Tourism at the forefront of promoting ecotourism – a concept that encourages environmental conservation along with tourism development.

Up until a decade ago, the Philippines, a biodiversity treasure trove, was in danger of losing much of its rainforest and coral reefs due to massive logging and dynamite fishing. The distinctly unique flora and fauna of the country were slowly disappearing. Conservation programmes funded both by foreign and local sources were initiated to preserve the natural environments and avert an ecological downtrend. It will take an enormous and sustained effort from both government and the private sector to succeed in this massive undertaking.

I am happy therefore to have the opportunity to write the foreword for this extremely interesting book with its stunning photographs and extensive information to guide the reader through the National Parks and Other Wild Places of the Philippines. I believe that it will achieve its aim to bring to closer public awareness the dangers posed to our natural resources and will show how to protect our rich environment for future generations.

I would like to congratulate the author Nigel Hicks for his excellent photographs and his exhaustive research work done on the biogeographical development of the Philippines, and also Jack Jackson for his colourful underwater photography and the publisher, New Holland, for producing one of the best books on biodiversity in the Philippines.

GCaraneta

Gemma Cruz-Araneta
Secretary of Tourism

INTRODUCTION

The Philippines is a widely-flung archipelago sitting at the eastern edge of Asia, the South China Sea to the west and the vast expanses of the Pacific Ocean to the east. It is a rugged landscape, most of the islands creased into mountain ranges and volcanoes, their slopes cloaked in dense rainforests, their shores-lined with mangroves and coral reefs. Although a tropical country at sea level, climbing into the mountains brings one into an increasingly temperate climate, with cool days and chilly nights.

Having risen up out of the sea, most of the Philippine islands have never been in contact with mainland Asia, and as a result have developed their own unique fauna and flora, which makes this country a treasure trove of potential new biological discoveries. Many of the animals of the coastal coral reefs, on the other hand, are similar to those encountered across much of the Indo-Pacific region. Nevertheless, the Philippines has one of the world's richest reef faunas, with well over 400 species of corals identified so far.

A network of protected areas makes it possible to visit a wide range of natural environments, from high mountain peaks to deep coral reefs, from rough volcano slopes to dense rainforests. Many of these areas are home to some unusual wildlife, from the spectacularly colourful sea fans of the coral reefs to the gigantic Almaciga trees and the rare Philippine Eagle of the rainforests.

A Sprawling Archipelago

The Philippine islands cover a vast area, stretching more than 1,200 kilometres (750 miles) from north to south

Left: Dense rainforest on Mt Kitanglad, Mindanao, a favourite haunt of the Philippine Eagle.
Above: The endangered Blue-naped Parrot is one of many bird species endemic to the Philippines.

and over 750 kilometres (470 miles) east to west at their widest point. There are no land borders; the nearest that any of the islands come to other countries are the Batanes Islands in the far north, less than 200 kilometres (124 miles) from Taiwan, Tawi-Tawi in the far south, just 35 kilometres (22 miles) from the east coast of Borneo, and Bal-abac Island at the southern tip of Palawan, which lies about 50 kilometres (31 miles) from Borneo's north coast.

There are said to be 7,107 islands, although more than half are too small even to have a name. The largest 10 islands make up over 90 per cent of the total land area of 300,000 square kilometres (116,000 square miles), with Luzon in the north and Mindanao in the south comprising two-thirds of this area. Between these two are several clusters of smaller islands, known collectively as the Visayas, while just to their north lies the rugged island of Mindoro. The country's westernmost fringe is marked by Palawan, a long, pencil-shaped island that is renowned for being still wild and thinly populated.

The Philippines' Biogeographical Development

It is believed that the Philippines started to form about 50 million years ago, when islands far to the east and south of the country's present location were gradually pushed west and north by the migrating Australasian tectonic plate. These islands began to coalesce into the Philippines when they became increasingly compressed against the Eurasian plate, causing new land to be created by a combination of volcanic activity and up-lifting.

It is a process that continues today – the small Philippine tectonic plate still being squeezed between the much larger Eurasian and Australasian plates – continually driving the Philippines' mountains higher, causing frequent earthquakes and volcanic eruptions. Volcanoes are a dominant feature of the Philippine landscape, there being an estimated 200, with 22 presently classed as active.

Although much of the country has risen up out of the sea and is believed never to have had direct contact with any major landmass, there are two exceptions: Palawan and Mindoro. The former is thought to have started life attached to southern China before migrating to its present location 17–40 million years ago. It is believed that the northern third of Mindoro made the same journey, but that its southern two-thirds migrated from Borneo.

The Philippine islands' long-term isolation has ensured the development of a unique fauna and flora. Moreover, even within the Philippines many of the different island groups have been isolated from each other for so long that quite large species differences now exist among them. Lower sea levels during successive ice ages have allowed exchange of plants and animals among some islands but not others, giving rise to several major biogeographical zones that can be distinguished by the presence or absence of certain indicator species. The most recent ice age occurred 15,000–20,000 years ago, when sea levels around the Philippines were 120 metres (394 feet) lower than today. At that time the country contained five major islands, and although today higher sea levels have reduced them to clusters of smaller islands, their original form can still be recognized by mapping out areas where the sea is less than 120 metres (394 feet) deep. The resulting five identifiable areas are now considered the Philippines' major faunal regions.

These are known as Greater Luzon, (covering much of the northern half of the country), Mindoro, Palawan, Greater Mindanao (consisting of Mindanao and the Visayan islands of Bohol, Samar and Leyte), and the Western and Central Visayas (also known as the Greater Negros-Panay Faunal Region, consisting of the islands of Panay, Negros, Guimaras, Cebu and Masbate). Several small island clusters maintain their own biogeographic zones, having remained isolated even during periods of such low sea levels. These include the Sulu Islands in the south, the Batanes Islands in the north and Sibuyan Island in the Visayas.

Palawan is quite distinct from the rest of the Philippines, its fauna and flora closely related to those of Borneo. This is due to the two having once been connected by a land bridge, and to the presence of the Wallace Line. Running between Palawan and the rest of the Philippines, the Wallace Line is one of the world's most important biogeographic divisions, named after the 19th-century British biologist who identified it. Running roughly north–south, it marks a major boundary between Asiatic species to the west (including Palawan) and a progressively more Australasian fauna and flora to the east. Most of the Philippines, lying immediately east of the line, sits above an area known as Wallacea, a transitional zone in which the fauna and flora show both Asian and Australasian characteristics. The Philippines received some of its founding fauna and flora from Wallacea via Sulawesi, some from Borneo through Palawan, and some from northeast Asia via Taiwan and the Batanes, so its wildlife represents a remarkable mix of origins.

A Unique Fauna and Flora

The result of this complex biogeographic history is a unique, highly diverse and confusing plant and animal wildlife that has rendered the Philippines one of the world's most important biodiversity hotspots. Of the country's 556 bird species, for example, 44 per cent are unique, or endemic, to the country. For mammals, the number is even higher – 111, or 67 per cent, out of 180

Below: As a sprawling archipelago, water features prominently in the landscape, from dramatic waterfalls, such as Katibawasan Falls, on Camiguin Island, Mindanao (left), to beautiful island-studded bays, such as El Nido in Palawan (right).

species – while for reptiles, amphibians and higher plants the rate of endemism is believed to be as much as 75 per cent. With the exception of birds, much of this fauna and flora has only recently started to come under serious scientific scrutiny, with the result that new species are being discovered at a faster rate than in any other country apart from Brazil, a vastly larger place.

Most mammals are rather small, mainly bats and small rodents, with many of the latter having extremely restricted ranges. One of the few large mammals is the Tamaraw, a dwarf buffalo that lives only on Mindoro. Others are the Philippine Tarsier, the world's smallest primate, and the Philippine Flying Lemur – both Philippine endemics restricted to Greater Mindanao (Mindanao and adjacent islands). Other mammals include several species of deer, one of which is spread across much of the country, while another – the Visayan Spotted Deer – is restricted to the islands of the Negros-Panay region. There are also several species of wild pig, again most of them showing very restricted ranges.

Palawan is the one part of the Philippines that is home to a range of mammals that are also found in other parts of Southeast Asia. These include the Binturong, or Bearcat, Asian Short-clawed Otter and Mouse Deer, all animals found in no other part of the Philippines.

The grandest of all the Philippine endemic animals, however, is undoubtedly the Philippine Eagle, which with a height of over one metre (three feet), is the world's second biggest eagle, beaten only on weight by the Harpy Eagle of South America. Today it lives on in the remoter forests of northern Luzon, Samar and Mindanao.

Around the coasts are an estimated 34,000 square kilometres (13,000 square miles) of coral reefs, home to over 450 species of coral and 400 of fish. A healthy reef is a stunningly complex array of corals that range from huge rock-like plates to tiny delicate tree-like translucent structures. A vast array of multi-coloured fish use the reef as a home, shelter and feeding area, while around those reefs that are close to deepwater shoals of pelagic fish are common, including barracuda, tuna, jacks and sharks. Some of the remoter reefs are frequented by several species of marine turtle, while whales and dolphins can be seen in the deeper waters offshore. A few areas, mainly around Palawan, have small populations of the Dugong, or Sea Cow, a strange-looking marine mammal that feeds on seagrass.

Conserving the Philippines' Natural Riches

Almost all of the Philippines' terrestrial fauna and flora are adapted to life in the rainforest, meaning that their survival depends on healthy forests. The country had one of Asia's first protected areas systems, established in the early 1930s, but following the Second World War massive logging operations paid little heed to park boundaries, and there was scant attempt to enforce their protection. By the late 1980s old-growth forest cover was down to an estimated 24,000 square kilometres (9,000 square miles), less than 10 per cent of the forest believed to have existed at the end of the 19th century.

It was at the end of the 1980s that international scientists and conservationists became aware of the enormous pool of biodiversity that existed in the Philippines, much of it by this time endangered. Plans were laid to start a major new conservation initiative, aiming to protect examples of every habitat in each of the country's major faunal regions. The programme began with a debt-for-nature swap in which a number of important protected areas

Below: *The majority of the population lives along the coast, where fishing boats are a common sight, such as along the coast of Panay (left). Mangroves have been greatly damaged, but some are now undergoing restoration, such as at Baclayon on Bohol (right).*

were put in the care of the World Wide Fund for Nature (WWF) in return for cancellation of some of the country's debts. This was followed in 1992 with a nationwide ban on logging and the promulgation of the National Integrated Protected Areas System (NIPAS) Law.

Ten sites vital to conservation and located in different biogeographical zones were selected as priority protected areas, to be given extra-special care largely funded by the World Bank. This has been backed up by a European Union initiative, which, with its National Integrated Protected Areas Programme (NIPAP), has set out to look after a further eight areas. These 18 sites now form the backbone of the country's Integrated Protected Areas System (IPAS). In addition, there is a plethora of sites left over from the old protected areas system. Many of these are still worth protecting, and are benefiting from the increased profile that Philippine conservation in general is receiving. All these protected areas are managed by the Protected Areas and Wildlife Bureau (PAWB), a branch of the Department of Environment and Natural Resources (DENR), although there is also considerable input from overseas experts, particularly at the NIPAP sites.

Although included within the IPAS, Palawan has also developed its own protected areas system, a result of the entire province being declared a biosphere reserve by UNESCO in 1990. This paved the way for the establishment of an Environmentally Critical Areas Network (ECAN), within which the most environmentally important sites have been declared protected areas. Much of this work is overseen by the Palawan Council for Sustainable Development (PCSD), a quasi-government body, although NIPAP is also involved in several IPAS sites.

Around the coast, a number of the larger coral reefs have been included within either the IPAS or Palawan's ECAN. In addition, local marine reserves are being established all over the country, set up by alliances of fishermen, local government and environmental campaign groups. Although these are designed in the first instance to help local communities boost their fish yields, this is being achieved through protection and hence restoration of damaged and over-fished coral reefs.

People of the Protected Areas

Many of the protected areas contain or are surrounded by rural communities, largely Christian lowland Filipinos, but in remote and upland regions often one or more of the country's 30 or so cultural minorities. In Luzon the most commonly encountered of the latter are the Negritos, usually thought of as the Philippines' aborigines, who still live a largely nomadic life within the forests.

Other minorities that one is likely to meet include the Ivatans, who live in the Batanes Islands, the Manobo in southeastern Mindanao, the Mangyan across much of Mindoro, and the Tagbanua in northern Palawan. All speak their own languages, have their own cultural traditions, and usually consider the protected area in which they live an essential part of their ancestral domain, something that has had to be carefully considered in establishing the IPAS.

Visiting the Protected Areas

To visit any of the country's terrestrial protected areas is to step into a primeval world of dense, tangled forests,

Below: *The wildlife is unusual and varied, ranging from the almost ubiquitous Long-tailed Macaque (centre) to the rare White-winged Flying Fox (left) and the Philippine Hawk-eagle (right).*

twisted trees covered in a mass of ferns, orchids and wet moss. This is the world of the Philippine rainforest, much of it located on the steep slopes of volcanoes, some inactive, others still smouldering and continually in danger of erupting. For the hiker, these mountains offer some of the most challenging and rewarding terrain.

Around the coast, the reefs provide some of the most stunning diving opportunities anywhere in Southeast Asia, large areas teeming with fish life. The most accessible of the reefs are served by well equipped and knowledgeable dive operators, who can provide a very worthwhile diving experience.

All the protected areas included in this book are of importance to conservation, and have been divided up into chapters that coincide with the country's five major faunal regions. All are open to the public, although some may require a permit. While most of the marine sites are well served by dive operators, at many of the terrestrial parks and reserves facilities are spartan to say the least, although plans exist to develop ecotourism services at many. Almost all the forest parks do contain paths, but signposting is usually absent so it is essential to hire a local guide. Obtaining written information about many of the parks can be difficult, but staff at each protected area office are very helpful and can normally provide a guide. For those areas where hiking is being actively promoted, the local tourist office may also be able to help.

Watching Wildlife and Other Activities

When visiting forested protected areas, looking for mammals and birds can be difficult. The vegetation is usually extremely dense and most Philippine animals are very small. Nevertheless, forest birds can usually be found early in the morning, especially in places where the canopy is open. Almost everyone visiting the forests of Mindanao or northern Luzon dreams of spotting a Philippine Eagle, although the chances of doing so are very small. Fortunately, the Philippine Eagle Nature Center, near Davao, provides the opportunity to come really very close to this magnificent bird. With the exception of macaques, finding mammals can be even harder, although with the aid of a local guide the daytime roosts of fruit bats, for example, can be found.

Looking for plants obviously provides an opportunity to get close to your subjects. Searching for those of greatest interest requires attention to detail and an ability to pick out subjects from the tangle of vegetation. In time, orchids, unusual ferns, pitcher plants and colourful fungi reveal themselves to the watchful.

Beneath the sea things could hardly be more different! Here you are confronted with a vast array of life – corals, starfish, large and small fish, lobsters – almost none of which flee at your approach. This is wildlife watching at its best, simply because it is so straightforward and varied.

One of the greatest pleasures in exploring the protected areas of the Philippines is the chance to experience the natural world in all its diversity, from montane and lowland rainforests through mangrove and marshes to splendid coral reefs and coralline islands. Here one encounters a huge range of life from tiny crabs and spiders to whales and gigantic trees, all adding up to a tremendous insight into the immense beauty of our planet. It is an experience that can only drive home just how essential it is for us to ensure that these treasures survive forever.

Below: *While much of the land is under pressure from the ever-growing rural population (left), the coast still offers such beautiful sights as palm-lined beaches (centre), and stunning submarine coral reefs (right).*

The National Parks and Other Wild Places of The Philippines

KEY

─────	Main road
─ ∙ ─ ∙ ─	International boundary
Manila ○	City or major town
Puerto Galera ○	Village or small town
Agusan	Water feature
Mt Pulag 2930m ▲ (9613ft)	Peak in metres (feet)
✈	International airport
✦	Domestic airport

0	100	200	300	400	500	600 km

0	50	100	150	200	250	300	400 miles

MALAYSIA

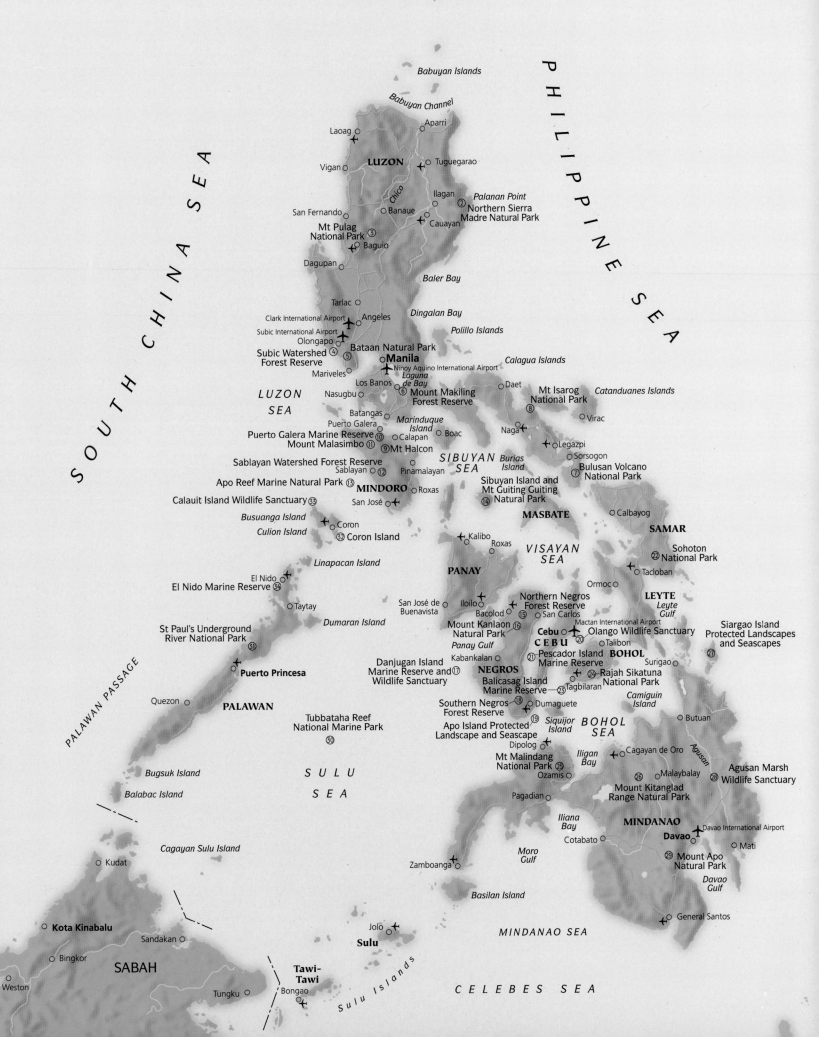

Itbayat Island
Batanes Islands
Protected Landscapes ①
and Seascapes ✈ Batan Island

Babuyan Islands

Babuyan Channel

Laoag ○   Aparri ○
        ✈
Vigan ○   **LUZON**   ○ Tuguegarao
                    ✈
                Ilagan ○   Palanan Point
San Fernando ○   Chico   ② Northern Sierra
        ○ Banaue   Madre Natural Park
Mt Pulag ③   ✈ Cauayan
National Park
    ✈ ○ Baguio
Dagupan ○   Baler Bay

Tarlac ○   Dingalan Bay

Clark International Airport ✈ ○ Angeles   Polillo Islands
Subic International Airport ✈
Olongapo ○   Bataan Natural Park   Calagua Islands
Subic Watershed ④ ⑤   ○ **Manila**
Forest Reserve   ✈ Ninoy Aquino International Airport
Mariveles ○   Los Banos ○   Laguna   ○ Daet   Mt Isarog
        de Bay   ⑥ Mount Makiling   National Park
Nasugbu ○   Forest Reserve   ⑧   ○ Virac
    Batangas ○   Marinduque   ○ Naga ✈   Catanduanes Islands
    Puerto Galera ○   Island   Legazpi
Puerto Galera Marine Reserve ⑩ ○ Calapan   ○ Boac   ○ Sorsogon
Mount Malasimbo   ⑨ Mt Halcon   **SIBUYAN**   Burias   ⑦ Bulusan Volcano
Sablayan Watershed Forest Reserve   **SEA**   Island   National Park
    Sablayan ○ ⑫   Pinamalayan ○   Sibuyan Island and
Apo Reef Marine Natural Park ⑬   Mt Guiting Guiting
Calauit Island Wildlife Sanctuary ㉝   **MINDORO**   ○ Roxas   ⑭ Natural Park
        San José ○   **MASBATE**   ○ Calbayog

Busuanga Island   **VISAYAN**   **SAMAR**
Culion Island   ✈ ○ Coron   ✈ ○ Kalibo   **SEA**   Sohoton
        ㉜ Coron Island   ○ Roxas   ㉒ National Park
                    Ormoc ○   ✈ ○ Tacloban
Linapacan Island   **PANAY**   **LEYTE**
El Nido ○   Leyte
El Nido Marine Reserve ㉞   San José de ○   ✈   Northern Negros   Gulf
            Buenavista   Iloilo ○   Forest Reserve   Siargao Island
        ○ Taytay   Bacolod ✈   Mactan International Airport   Protected Landscapes
Dumaran Island   Mount Kanlaon   ⑮ ○ San Carlos   ✈   and Seascapes
St Paul's Underground   Natural Park ⑯   **Cebu**   Olango Wildlife Sanctuary
River National Park   Panay Gulf   **CEBU** ⑳   ○ Talibon   ㉗
        ㉛   Kabankalan ○   ㉑ Pescador Island   **BOHOL**   ○ Surigao
    ✈   Marine Reserve
    Puerto Princesa   Danjugan Island   ㉔ Rajah Sikatuna
            Marine Reserve and   **NEGROS**   National Park
Quezon ○   Wildlife Sanctuary ⑰   Balicasag Island ㉓ Tagbilaran   Camiguin
        PALAWAN   Marine Reserve   Island
            ○ Dumaguete   **BOHOL**   ○ Butuan
        Tubbataha Reef   Southern Negros ⑱   **SEA**
        National Marine Park   Forest Reserve   ⑲ Siquijor
                Apo Island Protected   Island
    ㉚   Landscape and Seascape   ○ Dipolog   Cagayan de Oro ○
                    Mt Malindang   Iligan   ✈
            SULU   National Park ㉕   Bay   ○ Malaybalay   Agusan Marsh
        Bugsuk Island   ○ Ozamis ㉖   ㉘ Wildlife Sanctuary
            SEA   Pagadian ○   Mount Kitanglad
    Balabac Island   Range Natural Park
                    Iliana   **MINDANAO**
Cagayan Sulu Island   Bay   Cotabato ○   ✈ Davao International Airport
        Zamboanga ○   Moro   **Davao** ○ ○ Mati
○ Kudat   Gulf   ㉙ Mount Apo
Sandakan ○   National Park
○ Bingkor   **SABAH**   Basilan Island   Davao
                                Gulf
Weston ○   Jolo ○   ✈ ○ General Santos
            Sulu
    Tawi-   ○   **MINDANAO SEA**
    Tawi   Sulu Islands
Tungku ○ ✈ Bongao   **CELEBES SEA**

Kota Kinabalu

SOUTH CHINA SEA

PHILIPPINE SEA

LUZON SEA

PALAWAN PASSAGE

LUZON

Luzon is the largest of the Philippines' islands, with an area of approximately 105,000 square kilometres (40,000 square miles). The northern half forms the main body of the island, while the south, known as Bicol, consists of a long peninsula stretching southeastwards. There are also numerous island groups, such as the Polillo Islands off the east coast, Catanduanes in Bicol, and the Batanes beyond Luzon's far northern tip.

The south consists of the Calabarzon region and the long Bicol peninsula. Both are volcanic, with four active and numerous dormant volcanoes between them. Northern Luzon, on the other hand, consists of two large plains and three major mountain ranges, the latter consisting of the Zambales Mountains, the Cordillera Central and the Sierra Madre. The first is a chain running along the west coast. The Cordillera Central occupies much of the northcentral and northwestern regions. Many mountains here are over 2,000 metres high, including Mount Pulag, Luzon's highest, allowing pine forests to thrive. The Sierra Madre runs along about 500 kilometres (310 miles) of the east coast and remains wild and remote, supporting large areas of lowland rainforest.

The protected areas of Luzon consist almost entirely of forested mountains. The one exception is Batanes, a wild and remote island group lying far to the north. On the mainland the Northern Sierra Madre Natural Park, the country's largest protected area, encompasses remote coastal forest, while in the Cordillera Central Mount Pulag offers one of Luzon's best mountain hiking opportunities. At the southern end of the Zambales Mountains, Subic Watershed Forest is one of Luzon's few remaining tracts of lowland dipterocarp rainforest and is one of the best places in the country to get close to wildlife. The southern half of Luzon offers several volcanic protected areas, among which Mounts Makiling, Isarog and Bulusan are described here.

BATANES PROTECTED LANDSCAPES AND SEASCAPES

A Rugged Outpost

One of the remotest parts of the country, the Batanes Islands lie nearly 300 kilometres (190 miles) north of the nearest point on the Philippine mainland, yet less than 200 kilometres (120 miles) south of Taiwan. Surrounded by stormy seas, with the South China Sea to the west and the Pacific Ocean to the east, the islands are renowned for their rugged beauty – sheer cliffs alternating with rocky beaches, the inland areas a mixture of pastures and stunted forests.

Altogether there are 10 islands, although only three of them – Batan, Sabtang and Itbayat – are inhabited, making up a total land area of 23,000 hectares (57,000 acres), but surrounded by an estimated 450,000 hectares (1.1 million acres) of territorial waters. Together the Batanes Islands comprise the

Philippines' smallest province and the only one to be wholly designated a protected area. Proclaimed in 1994 and protected for their mix of stunning scenery, important wildlife and unique cultural environment, the islands comprise one of the country's 10 new priority protected areas, part of the Integrated Protected Areas System (IPAS) that is being funded by the World Bank.

A Land of Rolling Vistas

The main island, Batan, 19 kilometres (12 miles) long and barely five kilometres (three miles) wide at its widest point, consists mostly of high rolling hills, though the northernmost area is dominated by the sweeping contours of volcanic Mount Iraya (1,008 metres/3,307 feet). The provincial capital, Basco, sits at Iraya's feet, occupying what little flat land the island has. Batan's second highest point is Mount Matarem (459 metres/1,506 feet), situated in the south of the island.

Batan's coast consists of a series of alternating cliffs and rocky bays, some of the latter occupied by rustic villages. One of the most interesting beaches is that at San Joaquin, in Valugan Bay, where the entire shore is lined by large, almost perfectly round boulders.

Off Batan's southwest coast is the much smaller Sabtang, characterized by a coastline similar to that of Batan, but with a rugged inland terrain of small, steep hills. To the north lies Itbayat, largest of the Batanes Islands, but lightly populated and rarely visited. With no harbours, natural or man-made, and completely ringed

Opposite above: Mt Iraya, one of the country's 22 active volcanoes dominates the northern end of Batan Island.

Opposite below: Offshore rocks stand silhouetted by a setting sun, a view typical of Batan, main island in the Batanes group.

Above right: A farmer on Sabtang Island poses in his kanaye rain cape.

Previous pages:
Page 20: Malabsay Falls, surrounded by dense forest, cascades down Mt Isarog in the south of Luzon. Page 21: An iridescent Damselfly alights on waterside vegetation, in Bataan Natural Park.

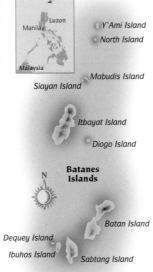

Luzon
Manila
Malaysia
Siayan Island
Y'Ami Island
North Island
Mabudis Island
Itbayat Island
Diogo Island
Batanes Islands
N
Dequey Island
Ibuhos Island
Batan Island
Sabtang Island

Location: Approx 290 km (180 miles) north of Aparri, the northernmost town in Luzon, and 190 km (118 miles) south of the southern tip of Taiwan.

Climate: There is no distinct dry season, although March to May are usually the sunniest. December to February are cooler but may also be quite wet. From June to November the islands are frequently swept by typhoons.

When to go: The islands are only reliably accessible from March to May. During the rest of the year access will be very variable, according to the weather.

Access: Three flights a week to Basco from Manila by Laoag Airlines, changing plane in either Laoag or Tuguegarao, in northern Luzon. There is no ferry service.

Permits: Not required.

Equipment: Good walking shoes, windproof and rainproof clothing, plus binoculars for birdwatching.

Facilities: Accommodation consists of three simple guesthouses in Basco. Public transport around Batan is limited, though a few jeepneys can be hired. An intermittent ferry runs from Ivana at the southern end of Batan to Sabtang. There is no regular connection to Itbayat. Guides may be hired; ask at your guesthouse or the protected area headquarters, in Basco.

Watching wildlife: A variety of birds can be seen, especially in the forested areas. Watch out for the Grey-faced Buzzard during the migration season. The seashore often has some interesting flowers, while inland the Voyavoy palm is quite common.

Visitor activities: Hiking, birdwatching, landscape photography

Above: *A type of begonia growing on the upper sea shore in Mananioy Bay on the east coast of Batan.*

Below: *A butterfly in lowland rainforest at the base of Mt Iraya, Batan.*

forest is the larger and more intact, its trees are more stunted due to wind exposure. The lower levels, 200–500 metres (650–1,600 feet) above sea level, consist of lowland evergreen rainforest, while at 500–800 metres (1,600–2,600 feet) lower montane rainforest is found. Above 800 metres (2,600 feet) is grassland only.

The islands, especially the forested areas, are a vital part of the east Asian flyway for migrating birds, the months of April and October being particularly important for flocks heading northwards and southwards, respectively. The largest flocks can be seen in October, although this is unfortunately a time when the islands are likely to be inaccessible due to bad weather. Fewer birds are seen during the April migrations, but one regularly encountered is the Grey-faced Buzzard, which passes through the Batanes Islands on its way to Taiwan and Japan.

by cliffs, landing places are few and far between, making visits difficult in all but the calmest conditions.

Habitats and Wildlife

On account of its remoteness from the Philippine mainland, Batanes forms a distinct biogeographic zone, its fauna and flora transitional between those of the Philippines and Taiwan. Inland, most of the natural vegetation is lowland evergreen rainforest, with today a little less than 6,000 hectares (14,900 acres), or about one quarter of the total land area, given over to this habitat.

Most forest is found on Itbayat and the western side of Sabtang, although in both of these areas there have been few studies. On Batan there are two forests, on the slopes of Mount Matarem and Mount Iraya. While Iraya's

The People of Batanes

The islands' 15,000 inhabitants are almost all members of the Ivatan cultural minority, a group which can be found only in Batanes. Speaking their own distinct tongue, they are thought to be pure descendants of Austronesian immigrants who arrived here from Taiwan or southern China about 4,000 years ago, right at the start of their long odyssey of expansion that led them to inhabit much of Southeast Asia and the Pacific islands.

With these islands inaccessible for large parts of the year, the Ivatans lead a life of self-sufficiency, characterized by subsistence farming and inshore fishing. Cultural traditions remain strong, especially in the remoter areas, such as on Sabtang Island. Here, traditional rain capes, called *soot* for women and *kanaye* for men, are still woven from fibres of the Voyavoy palm, a small squat type of palm tree that grows widely in the rugged terrain.

Invigorating trails

The main activity for the visitor is hiking. There are a number of trails, and perhaps the most obvious being the ascent of Mount Iraya. Starting close to the airport's runway, the path climbs steeply through dense forest, before emerging into grassland at a shoulder on the mountain's upper slopes. The hike up and down requires a day and should be started early in the morning in order to beat the cloud that inevitably builds up on Iraya's summit. It is important to take a guide.

Other hikes on Batan include walks along the northwestern cliffs above Basco, the main town, and over the

hills around Mount Matarem in the south of the island. On Sabtang, it is possible to hike right around the island, a route that will take in some very rugged scenery, and along the way pass through a number of old villages, built with massively thick stone walls and roofed with thatch. It is in places such as these that cape-weaving and boat-building can often be seen.

Above: *Lowland rainforest cloaks the lower slopes of Mt Iraya, greatly stunted by the fierce winds that sweep across the Batanes Islands.*

Right: *Close to the village of San Joaquin the beach that lines Valugan Bay is composed of thousands of rounded boulders, shaped by years of erosion by surf.*

Below: *Offshore rocks at low tide, a view typical of Batan, main island in the Batanes group.*

NORTHERN SIERRA MADRE NATURAL PARK

A Vast Forest Wilderness

At almost 360,000 hectares (890,000 acres) this is the country's largest protected area, encompassing a rugged and enormous tract of tropical lowland rainforest, which stretches along the isolated northeast coast of Luzon within Isabela province. The forest's remoteness has enabled it to escape the unwelcome attention of loggers. Consequently it remains one of the country's last great wilderness areas – barely explored, let alone studied or scientifically described – and is of international significance as the only known home of the Philippine Eagle within Luzon. A huge and largely still unknown reservoir of biodiversity, the park was established in 1997 as an essential component in the new World Bank-funded Integrated Protected Areas System (IPAS).

Opposite above: Wading along a river, near Palanan town, often the only way to walk through the Sierra Madre's lowland forests.

Opposite below left: The large butterfly, Lucaena idea, is common in woodland areas.

Opposite below middle: The red flowers of Clerodendrum make for a vivid splash of colour on the edge of a forest clearing near Palanan town.

Opposite below right: Although highly endangered, the mighty Philippine Eagle, the world's second largest eagle, lives on in the forests of the Northern Sierra Madre.

Above right: Park rangers guide their boat into Port Dimalansan

A Little-Known Region

The east coast of Luzon, from its northernmost tip to Quezon province over 500 kilometres (300 miles) to the south, is isolated from the rest of the island by a chain of mountains, the Sierra Madre. This range is divided into the Northern and Southern Sierra Madre by just one break, which occurs roughly at the midpoint of the range.

The Northern Sierra Madre mountains are wild and remote, with not a single road crossing the range in its entire length (although most maps do erroneously show several routes). Despite this isolation, many areas have been logged at least partially, although large areas within the newly declared natural park remain more or less untouched.

The terrain here is extremely rugged, the mountains steep and densely forested. The highest point within the park is Mount Cresta (1,672 metres/5,486 feet), with at least two more peaks over 1,000 metres (3,300 feet) high, namely Mounts Divilacan (1,311 metres/4,301 feet) and Palanan (1,212 metres/3,977 feet).

Three townships exist within the park's boundaries, Palanan, Divilacan and Maconacon, giving a total population of about 21,000. Many of these people are descendants of early settlers who migrated here during the 17th century. There is also a small population of Negritos, here known as Agta. They are members of the Philippines' aboriginal group and still live a largely

---

Location: Along the east coast of north-east Luzon, within Isabela province. The main town, Palanan, is about 74 km (46 miles) east-northeast of Cauayan, Isabela provincial capital, and 95 km (59 miles) south-east of Tuguegarao, capital of Cagayan province.

Climate: Tropical weather with high humidity and rainfall can be expected all year. The region is driest from March to May.

When to go: The weather is likely to be at its best from March to May, allowing air access and for boats to travel along the coast most of the time.

Access: Regular flights or daily buses from Manila to Tuguegarao. At Tuguegarao Airport report to the Chemtrad Aviation office and join the queue. Chemtrad's light aircraft run a shuttle service to Palanan and Maconacon when the weather is clear and there are enough passengers. Your itinerary must allow for delays.

Permits: Obtain from the natural park office in Cauayan (Cabatuan Rd, Cauayan). Visitors should also report to the Palanan police soon after arrival.

Equipment: Good walking shoes, cool clothing, camera, binoculars, torches, batteries insect repellent and anti-malarial prophylactics.

Facilities: Visitor facilities are very rudimentary. Accommodation consists of homestay; make arrangements with the natural park office in Cauayan or enquire on arrival in Palanan. Only very limited electricity even in Palanan township. Boats are available for hire; enquire at the riverside landing on the edge of town.

Watching wildlife: Spotting birds is difficult within the forest, but is possible along the rivers and in the mangroves. Bat roosts are known within the forest but are quite remote.

Visitor activities: Hiking, boating, birdwatching, photography.

Above: *A Negrito settlement on the beach inside Port Dimalansan, a popular site for these forest nomads.*

nomadic existence within the forest, their numbers inside the park have been variously estimated at between 400 and 1,300.

Inevitably, theirs is a subsistence livelihood, based on fishing and farming. Although there are also a few shops in Palanan, the Agtas essentially maintain a very basic hunter-gatherer lifestyle.

Conservation and Wildlife Studies

Although a few scientific expeditions were mounted into the Northern Sierra Madre mountains at the end of the 19th and in the early part of the 20th centuries, no truly comprehensive surveys were conducted until the 1990s.

Right: *Negrito women with their children, in Port Dimalansan.*

In 1991 and 1992 a large international team of scientists converged on the Palanan region in an attempt to ascertain both the condition of the forest and its biodiversity value. The results astonished even the most optimistic of workers. Bird studies revealed 241 species, nearly half of the entire country's species list, along with 78 of the nation's 169 endemic species, including the mighty Philippine Eagle, and 19 of the 25 species known to be restricted just to Luzon. It was a similar story with mammals, 14 species of bats being found, including six endemic to the Philippines. Similarly, nine species of rodent were found, all endemic. For larger mammals, one species each of deer, pig and monkey were found, along with two species of civet.

Studies of the forest's flora have barely begun, but it is likely that the diversity will be at least as great. Six kinds of forest have been identified, ranging from lowland evergreen rainforest, dominated by dipterocarp trees (which in areas exposed to the Pacific winds are much reduced from their normally gigantic heights), montane forest, mangroves, beach forest, limestone forest, and forest growing on ultrabasic rocks. The last of these consists of a stunted, specialized forest growing on land rich in phytotoxic heavy metals.

There have also been studies of the marine environment, which have revealed a number of healthy coral

reefs and extensive seagrass beds. Two species of turtle and the endangered Dugong have been sighted along this coast, and healthy fish populations are found offshore. The endangered Saltwater Crocodile is known to still live in the park's mangroves.

In 1997 the Palanan area became the country's largest protected area, with its boundaries based on the Palanan Wilderness, a protected area that had previously been declared in 1979 but which had in fact existed only on paper. The new park also includes a large marine component, designed to protect the reefs and fisheries, and taking up over 71,000 hectares (175,000 acres) of the park's 360,000 hectares (889,000 acres).

Penetrating the Wilderness

Access to the region can be quite difficult, but the reward for success is the sight of a wild and virtually pristine landscape, most easily viewed from the coast. The simplest route is to fly from Tuguegarao, capital of Cagayan province, to Palanan. The only alternative is a 30–40 hour boat ride from Baler, far to the south.

Exploration can be organized from Palanan town. One of the simplest journeys is to travel down the Palanan River to its mouth and the village of Sabang, from where it is a 90-minute walk through farmland

and forest, often wading upriver as the only route through the forest, to Sadsad Falls, a large cascade crashing into a pool in the midst of dense forest.

One of the best routes is to travel northwards by boat along the coast, stopping at the beautiful enclosed bay known as Port Dimalansan, and finishing at Maconacon. This route will not take you to any dense dipterocarp forest, but will include many stretches of pristine beach forest dominated by Barringtonia and Casuarina trees, plus the great expanse of mangroves within the most sheltered parts of Dimalansan. Agta communities are frequently based at beach sites within this bay but, since they move around, finding one can be a matter of luck. Although they rarely speak English, they will always give a friendly, if shy, welcome.

Top: *An overloaded boat ferries children across the Palanan River, on their way to school in Palanan town.*

Above right: *The Hooded Pitta scurries around on the forest floor, one of the 241 species of bird recently identified as living in the Northern Sierra Madre.*

Right: *Luzon Bleeding-heart Pigeons are found in the Northern Sierra Madre's forests as they are across Luzon.*

MOUNT PULAG NATIONAL PARK

Luzon's Highest Mountain

Located in northern Luzon's mountainous Cordillera Central, approximately 60 kilometres (37 miles) east of Baguio, this protected area encompasses Luzon's highest peak, the 2,930 metre (9,613 feet) Mount Pulag (often previously called Mount Pulog). Proclaimed a protected area in 1987, the rugged terrain, varying in altitude from 1,200 metres (3,940 feet) up to Pulag's summit and including 10 other summits over 2000 metres (6562 feet) high, incorporates a range of habitats that include pine forest, mossy forest and alpine grassland and covers an area of 11,500 hectares (28,400 acres). Although under pressure from encroaching farmland, Mount Pulag still protects some of Luzon's most important wildlife species, and for the visitor offers some of the country's best mountain hiking.

Opposite above: *The summit of Mt Pulag, Luzon's highest mountain, stands cloaked in mossy forest and ephemeral early morning mist.*

Opposite below left: *The Eye-browed Thrush is commonly seen in Mt Pulag's forest.*

Opposite below middle: *Wild raspberries, locally known as wild strawberries, flourish in Mt Pulag's mossy forest.*

Opposite below right: *During the winter months rhododendrons flower in many parts of the mossy forest, at altitudes of about 2000 metres (approximately 6,500 feet).*

Above right: *The gigantic Atlas Moth can be seen at night in the mountains of the Cordillera Central.*

Forested Mountains

The whole of the national park is characterized by very rugged terrain, with steep mountain slopes, gorges and ravines overlooked by prominent summits, some of them among the highest in the Philippines. Mount Pulag itself is the third highest in the country (though often claimed to be the second highest).

The lower slopes have a patchy covering of pine forest, composed entirely of a single species, Benguet Pine, one of only two species of pine found in the Philippines. In most of the park's accessible areas this pine forest was logged from the 1950s until 1972, so today almost all of it is secondary growth. Furthermore, many parts of the pine forest are now used for farming, and even in areas that still support dense stands of trees the undergrowth is often burned off to encourage the growth of new grass for animal grazing.

Above the pine forest, starting at an altitude of about 2,200 metres (7,200 feet), is the mossy forest, by far Pulag's dominant habitat. Covering an area of 5,800 hectares (14,300 acres), or about half of the national park, this consists of dense stands of small, gnarled trees, prominent among which are Philippine Oak, laurels and tree ferns, all of them draped in thick coverings of moss.

The tree-line is reached at about 2,600 metres (8,500 feet), and above this is a swathe of grassland. This is dominated by dwarf bamboo (a species common in the mountains of Taiwan), which on these exposed

Location: In the Cordillera Central mountains of northern Luzon, 60 km by road northeast of Baguio.

Climate: The area is dry and clear from November to mid-March, and rainy for the rest of the year. In January and February the summits may receive frost. It is always cold at night, with temperatures at Babadak just a few degrees above freezing.

When to go: It is advisable to climb Pulag only during the dry season, from November until the end of February.

Access: There is public transport from Baguio to Ambangeg, but it is rather limited. It is better to hire a vehicle. The usual route is to take the Ambuklao Road from Baguio, although it is also possible to travel from several points on the Halsema Road, via the town of Kabayan. Four-wheel-drive vehicles should be able to travel all the way to Babadak.

Permits: Obtainable at the Babadak ranger station.

Equipment: Tent, sleeping bag, cooking utensils, warm clothing, sturdy hiking shoes, camera and binoculars.

Facilities: The summit trail from Babadak is very easy to follow, though mostly not signposted. On the grassland a major divide in the path is signposted. There is a rest pavilion about 2 km above Babadak. There is flat ground for camping next to the Babadak ranger station and on the grassland.

Watching wildlife: There is little chance of spotting mammals in the dense forest, but birds can be commonly seen. In January and February many of the shrubs, such as azaleas and pieris, are in flower.

Visitor activities: Hiking, birdwatching, photography.

(Map labels: Luzon, Manila, Malaysia, IFUGAO, Mt Taboyo 2842m (9325ft), Kabayan, Kapangan, Mount Pulag National Park, Ranger Station, Ambangeg, BENGUET, Mt Pulag 2930m, Mt Babadak, Ranger Station, Ambaguio, Ambuklao Lake, La Trinidad, Baguio, NUEVA VIZCAYA, Binga Lake, Aritao)

Above: *Tree ferns are abundant in Philippine forests, mostly at the mid-altitude levels. Some hardy species thrive in the higher mossy forests, such as this cluster living at an altitude of about 2000 metres (approximately 6,500 feet).*

grasslands grows to a height of about 13 centimetres (five inches). In September, the grassland is vibrant with the colours of thousands of wild flowers.

Not surprisingly, most of the park's fauna is adapted to life in mossy forest, and includes such unique Philippine species as the Northern Giant Cloud-rat and the Bushy Cloud-rat, as well as numerous species of bat and a wide range of forest birds.

Conservation Work

With the first studies conducted as long ago as 1910, Mount Pulag's importance to biodiversity has long been appreciated. That early work revealed more than 500

Right: *The Philippine Deer, although rare, is spread across much of the country, and can be found in many protected areas, including Mt Pulag.*

Opposite: *Mt Pulag's mossy forest is characterized by stunted, gnarled trees draped in huge quantities of moss, soaking wet during most of the year, drying out only during part of the dry season.*

species of plant, of which 251 were Philippine endemics. A more recent bird survey identified 77 species, of which 13 have a very restricted distribution and eight are globally threatened.

In 1990 Mount Pulag National Park became one of five sites in the Philippines to become part of a debt-for-nature swap, administered for three years by the World Wide Fund for Nature. More recently, the park has been incorporated into the National Integrated Protected Areas Programme (NIPAP), a project funded and partly run by the European Union. Ranger stations have been established at the village of Ambangeg, at the foot of the mountain, and at Babadak, situated in the transition zone between pine and mossy forest. With rangers now permanently based at Babadak, it is hoped that wildlife studies and conservation enforcement can be carried out more effectively than has been possible in the past.

Hiking to the Summit

Mount Pulag has probably one of the best summit trails of any mountain in the Philippines, rendering it possible for climbers to hike without a guide.

The usual starting point is at Ambangeg, accessible from Baguio along an unmetalled road. It is important for hikers to bring all their supplies from Baguio as there is little available in Ambangeg. The first 10 kilometres (six miles) are up a steep track, passing by many vegetable farms and through areas of pine forest, to the ranger station at Babadak. Hikers with a four-wheel-drive vehicle can motor all the way to Babadak. Permits should be obtained from the ranger station before continuing on foot towards the summit, another 10 kilometres (six miles) away. It is a good idea to break the climb by camping overnight next to the ranger station. Anyone camping up here should realise that it gets very cold at this altitude (2,400 metres/7,874 feet), even in the Philippines, so it is important to be properly equipped.

From Babadak the trail, an old logging road, climbs towards a ridge where a rest hut sits at a divide in the trail. The path to the right leads to the summit, making its way along an enormous curving ridge, with a gentle climb through dense mossy forest, but frequently allowing clear views of Mount Pulag. Eight kilometres (five miles) from Babadak the path emerges from the forest and begins to cut across the grassland. The final scramble to the summit is rather steep and tiring, especially with the air now getting rather thin, but the reward is fabulous, windswept views of forest and mountains as far as the eye can see, pin-sharp in the clear mountain air.

SUBIC WATERSHED FOREST RESERVE

Lush Forests in an Old Naval Base

Situated 130 kilometres (80 miles) northwest of Manila and within the confines of what until 1992 was the USA's largest overseas naval base, the 10,000 hectare (24,700 acres) forest of Subic Bay is one of the Philippines' most accessible wilderness areas. Deliberately protected by the American military as a source of water, a security shield and for use in jungle survival training, the forest received a level of protection that could only be dreamed of for similar wilderness areas in the rest of the country.

When the navy pulled out the entire base and its 10,000 hectares (24,700) of forest became a special economic zone administered by the Subic Bay Metropolitan Authority (SBMA). Much of the base area has been turned into an industrial and commercial centre, but despite the obvious pressures this creates for nature conservation the Subic Watershed Forest Reserve remains one of the largest and healthiest surviving areas of lowland tropical rainforest in Luzon. It is contiguous with the forests of Bataan Natural Park,

Opposite: Mangroves in Triboa Bay, in the NavMag area of Subic Bay. The pneumatophores, or aerial roots, that surround the mangroves enable the trees to 'breathe' even when immersed in water.

Above right: The Northern Shoveler is amongst hundreds of ducks that visit the Triboa Bay mangroves during winter.

lying to the east and south, and these two areas – although still administered separately – have officially become part of the Subic-Bataan Natural Park, one of the country's 10 priority protected areas under the new IPAS programme.

Map

ZAMBALES — To Manila — N

Subic Bay — Olongapo — Subic Freeport — Olongapo Bay — Cubi Point — Subic International Airport — Pamulaklakin — Triboa Bay — Cubi — Jungle Environmental Survival Training Camp — **Subic Watershed Forest Reserve** — Naval Magazine (Nav Mag) — Binanga Bay — BATAAN

Luzon — Manila — Malaysia

Forests from Shore to Hill

Subic Bay is a large, deep inlet situated just north of Manila Bay, surrounded by hills, its mouth guarded by Grande Island. The topography along the eastern shore, where the economic zone is located, is quite gentle, backed by rolling hills. Most of the commercial and industrial area was cleared of trees long ago, but to the south the forest extends down to the edge of the airport, and encircles a number of residential areas, such as Cubi.

The main forested area lies still further south, however, in a region known as the Naval Magazine (today called simply NavMag), where there are still scores of underground bunkers once used to store ammunition. It is here that the forest cover reaches its most complete and impressive state, with mature stands of gigantic dipterocarp trees that stretch from the hills right down to the shore. Several of the small coves and river mouths are sites of extensive mangrove swamp, while the sandy shores are lined with beach forest, all of which merge with the dipterocarp forest immediately behind.

Although the forest is extensive and often dense, in places the canopy is quite open, there being a large number of dead trees. These were killed in 1991 by ash fallout from the eruption of nearby Mount Pinatubo. The forest is rapidly regrowing, but while the canopy remains open birdwatching is considerably easier than it would be in a wholly closed-canopy forest!

Teeming with Wildlife

As a result of the protection, the forest's wildlife is intact and relatively tame. Forest birds are especially abundant, and many species such as Stork-billed Kingfisher, Sooty Woodpecker, Lesser Tree Swift, Dollarbird, Blue-throated Bee-eater and even Luzon Hornbills are all readily visible from the many roads that cut through the forest. The mangroves within the NavMag area, particularly in Triboa Bay, teem with ducks, especially during the winter months, when hundreds of Philippine Mallard (an endemic bird) and the migratory Tufted Duck and

Left: *The Golden-crowned Flying Fox, one of the world's largest fruit bats, is one of the two species that make up the Subic fruit bat colony.*

Northern Shoveler can be seen. White-bellied Sea-eagles, Philippine Serpent-eagles and Brahminy Kites are all frequently and easily seen soaring above the forest canopy.

Long-tailed Macaques are also ubiquitous, often sighted sitting and feeding in family groups on the roadsides. Fruit bats are easily seen since a large colony roosts in tall trees close to Cubi. The thousands of bats that exist here consist of a mixture of the Philippine Giant Fruit Bat and the Golden-crowned Flying Fox, two of the world's largest bats, with a wingspan of up to two metres (six feet). The latter is endemic to the Philippines and highly endangered, so this site is of major importance to conservation.

Offshore, there are coral reefs around Grande Island and along the bay's outermost shores, while sharks, such as Blacktip Reef Sharks, patrol the inshore waters, and both Green and Olive Ridley Turtles still nest on a number of the beaches, including those along the very perimeter of the airport.

People of the Forest

Despite living within a military base, a population of Negritos, known as Aeta in this part of Luzon, were allowed to continue their existence in the forest. Today about 100 families still live here. No longer practising a fully hunter-gatherer existence, but engaged in farming and some aspects of the commercial economy, for years these people trained American soldiers for jungle survival. Today, they offer their skills to civilians as part of the SBMA's ecotourism programme, and can act as forest guides.

Forest Ecotourism

Subic Bay offers the visitor one of the most rewarding opportunities in the Philippines for a close encounter with a true wilderness area. The bat roost is easily viewed from a hillside lookout point right in Cubi, while anyone wishing to learn about jungle survival can take a special course from the Jungle Environmental Survival Training Camp (JEST). The men here offer visitors anything from a two-hour forest hike, during which a whole host of plants are pointed out and their uses demonstrated, to a week-long course. Nearby at Pamu-

Above right: *Some of the forest's biggest trees have huge buttress roots to support them in the shallow soil.*

Right: *Wild figs are plentiful in lowland rainforests such as Subic's and are a major food source for fruit bats.*

Above: *An Aeta tribesman living in the Subic forest demonstrates the traditional method of catching fish in the forest rivers.*

Right: *A member of JEST demonstrates how to make a rice steamer out of bamboo cut in the forest. All that is needed is the right knife.*

laklakin, the Aeta have established a model village where aspects of their traditional culture and lifestyle are demonstrated.

These three sites are outside the NavMag area and are easily accessible to the visitor. For trips into the NavMag it is necessary to obtain a permit from the SBMA's Ecology Centre and to have one of their forest rangers as a guide. A vehicle is also necessary, as public transport does not extend into the NavMag. In this region the main activity is hiking, and there are a variety of routes to be explored. Trails lead down to the mangroves of Triboa Bay, for example, or through the dipterocarp forest up to Hill 394, the highest point within the economic zone.

Opposite: *A Karpia tree, one of the giants of the lowland rainforest, but not a dipterocarp tree, towers through Subic's open canopy.*

BATAAN NATURAL PARK

Lowland Dipterocarp Forest

Situated about 100 km (60 miles) west-northwest of Manila, this park lies in the northern half of the Bataan Peninsula, a long projection of land that protects Manila Bay from the South China Sea. Covering an area of 23,700 hectares (58,500 acres), this is one of the few areas of lowland dipterocarp rainforest surviving in Luzon. Spread across an ancient volcanic landscape, with Mount Natib (1,253 metres/4,111 feet) as its highest point, the forests of Bataan are contiguous with those of the Subic Watershed Forest Reserve to the northwest. Declared a protected area in 1945, today the Bataan and Subic forests together make up the Subic-Bataan Natural Park, one of the Philippines' 10 priority protected areas under the new Integrated Protected Areas System (IPAS), although they remain administered separately. For the visitor, too, access points are far apart and the two forest areas feel quite different.

An Ancient Volcanic Landscape

Much of the park's terrain is quite rugged, consisting largely of the ancient Natib volcanic caldera estimated to be 7.5 kilometres (4¾ miles) north to south and 5.5 kilometres (3½ miles) east to west. Most of the park's mountain summits are arranged along the curving rim of the caldera, including Mount Natib itself. Other major peaks in the park include Bataan Peak (1,066 metres/3,498 feet), Mount Napundol (1,029 metres/3,376 feet), Mount Silanganan (910 metres/2,986 feet), Mount Nagpali (900 metres/2,953 feet) and Mount Santa Rosa (800 metres/2,625 feet). A number of hot springs exist within some of the remoter parts of the caldera, though none is especially hot. Exploration in the 1980s by the Philippine National Oil Corporation, in search of geothermal energy sources, concluded there was insufficient volcanic activity in the Natib caldera for geothermal energy extraction to be worthwhile.

Although partially logged in the 1970s, much of the park has remained relatively intact with about half of its area still covered by closed-canopy mature forest. The remainder is a mixture of secondary forest, scrub,

Opposite top: The dense lowland forest of Bataan Natural Park, clings to steep mountain slopes.

Opposite below left: Biologists take a break from inventory work, the arduous task of establishing just what the Philippines' protected areas actually contain.

Opposite below right: A small forest stream splashes down through the steep forested hills.

Above right: The Philippine Serpent-eagle is a common raptor in the country's forest areas, frequently seen soaring high above the trees.

Map labels: ZAMBALES · Luzon · Manila · Hermosa · Malaysia · Olongapo · Subic Freeport · Subic Bay · Subic Watershed Forest Reserve · Bataan Natural Park · Park Office · Mt Natib 1253m (4111ft) · Morong · BATAAN · Bagac · Bagac Bay · Cañas Point · LUZON SEA · Luzon Point · Mariveles · N · Corregidor Island · BATAAN PENINSULA · Samal · Abucay · Balanga · Pilar · Orion · Limay · Manila Bay · Cabcaben

Location: Within Bataan province, on Bataan Peninsula, about 100 km (60 miles) west-northwest of Manila.

Climate: Receives rain from the southwest monsoon, so is wet from June to October or November. Has a distinct dry season from November to May. May is the hottest month with temperatures up to 36°C (97°F). The coolest time is often during the rainy season, when temperatures may drop as low as 18°C (64°F).

When to go: Explore the park in the dry season, November–May. January is the best time as temperatures are at their most comfortable and humidity low.

Access: Frequent express buses run from Manila to Balanga and Abucay. Journey time is about three hours. From these towns, hire a jeepney to travel up to the park. Alternatively, self-drive car hire is available in Manila, making it possible to drive straight to the park. It will also make access to the west coast areas simpler.

Permits: Not required at present.

Equipment: Good walking shoes, camera, binoculars, full camping equipment for those intending to climb Mt Natib.

Facilities: At present very few visitor facilities. Nearest accommodation is in Balanga and Abucay. A few hiking trails exist. Guides can be hired; enquire at the park headquarters at the Balanga State College, Bangkal Abucay, or the park's non-government organization in Balanga.

Watching wildlife: Dipterocarp rainforest is common. Look for fruits on the forest trees, especially fig species, the staple diet for fruit bats. Serpent-eagles are often seen soaring overhead.

Visitor activities: Photography, birdwatching, hiking.

slash-and-burn farmland and grassland. While much of this forest is dipterocarp, on the mountains' higher levels this gives way to montane forest, and around the summit of Mount Natib is an area of mossy forest.

The western edge of the park runs along the Bataan Peninsula. It has some scenic bays and alternative access routes into the park's interior, but little forest.

People Within the Park

It is estimated that just over 1,000 households exist within the park's boundaries, including a very small number of Negrito Aeta families. Many of these people practise slash-and-burn farming around the forest's fringes, growing a mixture of vegetables, and with coffee and fruit orchards on permanently converted land.

Encroachment was greatly facilitated in the 1980s when the Philippine National Oil Corporation built tracks into the park while searching for geothermal energy sources. These tracks have now disintegrated and it is hoped that, with environmental protection, restoration of the damaged areas will be possible.

Fauna and Flora

To date, only limited studies have been conducted on the wildlife of the park, although it is expected to be much the same as that so far identified in the Subic Watershed Forest. Over 100 species of plants have been identified, but these cover mostly only the park's trees. The park's mammals are known to include Long-tailed Macaques, the Luzon Warty Pig, and several endemic species of rat, while birdlife is almost certain to be as extensive as that in the Subic Watershed Forest.

Above: *The Long-tailed Macaque, in the Philippines sometimes called the Philippine Macaque, is a common and ubiquitous animal, spread right across the country.*

Above right: *The Luzon Bleeding-heart Pigeon, although hard to find, lives in a number of Luzon's protected areas, including Bataan Natural Park.*

Right: *The Luzon version of the Rufous Hornbill is increasingly rare, but with luck it can be seen in the lowland forests of Bataan and Subic.*

Exploring the Park

Scant visitor infrastructure exists in Bataan Natural Park. The nearest accommodation is at Balanga, on the peninsula's east coast, about 10 kilometres (six miles) from the park's boundary. A few trails exist within the park, with one leading to the summit of Mount Natib. This is a steep route that passes through some of the park's best forest. Other paths explore the park's lower regions, passing through a mixture of forest and farmland, and passing by a number of beautiful waterfalls. It is essential to take a guide along on these trails. Enquire at the park office, located outside the Bataan State College, on the edge of the park near Bangkal Abucay.

The western side of the park is accessible from Balanga by road. From several points along here trails lead to waterfalls and attractive picnic areas.

MOUNT MAKILING FOREST RESERVE

A Much-studied Forest

Lying less than 60 km (37 miles) south of Manila and with a campus of the University of the Philippines on its lower slopes, this is one of the country's most studied forests. It also has one of the pleasantest aspects of any of the country's terrestrial protected areas. Mount Makiling itself is an inactive volcano rising up from the southern shores of Laguna de Bay, the Philippines' largest lake, and is approached through the pleasant and very leafy campus of the university, a prestigious institute located on the edge of the lakeside town of Los Banos, a place itself well known for its hot spring resorts.

Mount Makiling is one of the country's oldest protected areas, proclaimed a national park in 1933. Ever since, the forest has been under the management of the University of the Philippines, directly overseen by the Institute of Forest Conservation (IFC). Perhaps because of its small size, covering 4,200 hectares (10,500 acres), in 1993 the government downgraded Makiling's status from national park to forest reserve.

Fauna and Flora

Mount Makiling's great accessibility has long made it a centre for wildlife research. Indeed studies of its bird fauna began back in the 19th century, but research

Above right: The brilliant flowers of a lipstick plant are a common sight in Philippine forests, making a vibrant contrast against the greenery.

really picked up speed following establishment of the University of the Philippines' Los Banos campus. It is thanks to the involvement of the university that Mount Makiling's forest remains largely intact, at least on the northern slopes facing Los Banos. Here, the lower slopes up to an altitude of 600 metres (2,000 feet) still retain some areas of dipterocarp forest, some of the most accessible of which lie within the Mount Makiling Botanical Garden, situated right on the edge of the university campus. Despite being named a botanical garden, much of it consists simply of dense forest with good paths cut through it, name tags hammered onto many of the pathside tree-trunks to allow identification.

The higher slopes consist of montane forest, a dense forest with smaller trees and a tangle of lianas, palms, rattans and pandanus trees and climbers. Close to the summit at 1,144 metres (3,753 feet) the vegetation comes close to being mossy forest, characterized by a dense stunted forest, many of the trees draped in thick layers of moss.

The mammalian fauna is probably fairly limited due to the reserve's relatively small size, but it is known to contain Philippine Deer, cloud rats and Luzon Warty Pig. The reserve is unusual among Philippine protected areas in that its reptiles have been well studied, and have been found to consist of 70 species, most of them endemic to

---

Location: About 60 km (37 miles) south of Manila, on the southern shore of Laguna de Bay, the country's largest lake. Situated in Laguna province.

Climate: There is heavy rain from June to October, and lighter rain, especially on the mountain, from then until March. April and May are dry. Humidity is always high and temperatures may reach 36°C (96°F) during May.

When to go: To be assured of dry weather, visit in April or May. January–February are cooler, though there is likely to be some rain.

Access: Direct buses travel from Manila to Los Banos. From the town take a tricycle or jeepney to the campus. Jeepneys serve as public transport around the campus, but walking here is very pleasant.

Permits: Not needed, but if climbing the mountain register first with the guard on duty at the trailhead.

Equipment: Good walking shoes, waterproof clothing or umbrella, camera, binoculars, camping equipment if intending to stay on the mountain overnight.

Facilities: Excellent hotel accommodation is available in Los Banos. Botanical Garden has well-marked trails, with many species of tree labelled. The summit trail is clear, with diversions (e.g. to Mudsprings) well marked.

Watching wildlife: A wealth of bird species, most clearly visible on the campus. Look for Philippine Falconets in a tree beside the Institute of Forest Conservation.

Visitor activities: Hiking, birdwatching, visiting the Philippine Raptor Center, hot springs in Los Banos.

the Philippines. It is perhaps birds that have come in for the closest attention, with 241 species identified, almost half of them Philippine endemics.

Hiking and Birdwatching

Mount Makiling is one of the country's best-known birdwatching sites, attracting international birdwatchers who come to see the great range of Philippine endemics that this forest has to offer. Some of the best birdwatching is actually possible in the outer areas of the university campus, such as around the Institute of Forest Conservation (IFC) and the Botanical Garden, where trees are plentiful but the canopy is still sufficiently open for birds to be clearly visible.

For hikers, there is an excellent trail all the way to the summit. Starting at the outer edge of the university campus, right next to the IFC, this path was clearly once a road, ensuring that not only is it wide but gradients are relatively gentle. With such a clear path, this is one of the few occasions when hiking does not require a guide. The

Below left: *A Philippine Scops Owl, one of the many Philippine endemics to be found in Makiling's forest.*

Below: *An Emerald Dove, one of many pigeon species that inhabit the Philippines' forests and which can be seen at Makiling.*

now a mature and dense forest, the result of a forest restoration programme. Shortly beyond this point a small signposted trail leaves the main path and leads to an area called the Mudsprings. This is an area of boiling, steaming mud, hidden within the depths of the forest. This eerie sight is a reminder that, although sleeping, this is still a volcano and one that is far from dead. According to local scientists the Mudsprings have grown about 10-fold over the past 15 years, leading to fears in some quarters that volcanic activity may be increasing.

After returning to the main trail, the climb becomes steeper and the old road increasingly overgrown, although still wide by the standards of most forest paths. Eventually it will lead you to Peak Two, one of Makiling's three peaks, the ragged remains of a volcanic crater. Despite some clearance by campers in search of firewood the forest even on the summit is still quite dense, so there is little view from here.

The Botanical Garden is well worth a visit, not only for its taste of dipterocarp forest, but also because it is home to the Philippine Raptor Center, a small compound in the forest where a range of the country's raptor species are housed. Particularly impressive are two Philippine Eagles, truly massive birds, and a Philippine Serpent-eagle called Leila, so tame that she sits all day on an open-air perch and will allow even complete strangers to pick her up.

Below: *The beautiful flowers of* Couroupita guianensis, *high up in the tree canopy on the edge of the University of the Philippines campus.*

Above: *The Anglehead Lizard, one of the largest of Philippine lizards, climbing a tree in the lower montane forest on Makiling's slopes.*

round trip to the summit and back to the campus takes most of a day, and although the climb is not difficult be sure to carry plenty of water; even at high altitude it is warm and humid within the forest.

About one hour above the start of the trail one comes to the Makiling Rainforest Park, an open area within the forest for picnics, often used by school parties. Close by is a large plantation of Large-leaved Mahogany,

BULUSAN VOLCANO NATIONAL PARK

A Volcanic Lakeland

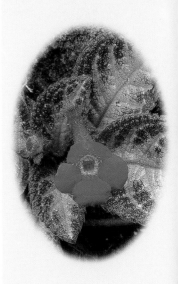

Mount Bulusan is one of three active volcanoes in the far south of Luzon, a region known as Bicol. Along with a number that are inactive, it is the southernmost member of the northwest–southeast Bicol Volcanic Chain, which also consists of Mounts Labo, Isarog, Iriga, Malinao and Mayon. At present, Mounts Bulusan, Iriga and Mayon are active in this chain.

Mount Bulusan is situated in Sorsogon province, the very southernmost toe of Luzon, about 60 kilometres (37 miles) south of Legaspi, the largest city in Bicol. The national park surrounding it, which was proclaimed in 1935, covers an area of 3,700 hectares (9,100 acres) and consists of a mixture of forest and grassland.

The Lie of the Land

The park lies close to a small town also called Bulusan, located on Sorsogon's east coast, and from here the land climbs steeply up through lush vegetation towards the volcano. The road that gives access to the park, a very quiet country lane, passes along the park's southern edge, connecting Bulusan town with the area's main centre, Irosin. The highest point in the park is the active crater of Mount Bulusan itself, at 1,559 metres (5,115 feet) above sea level, while other peaks include Mount Jormajam and Sharp Peak. In addition, there

Above right: The red Episcia flower, ground vegetation in a forest clearing close to Lake Bulusan.

are three lakes, the smallest, called Blackbird Lake, beside the active crater. Lake Aguingay nestles in a valley between Mount Bulusan and Sharp Peak, while the lowest (at an altitude of 600 metres/2,000 feet) and most accessible is Lake Bulusan. Covering just over 16 hectares (40 acres) this is also the largest of the lakes, and is the park's main access point, linked to the Irosin–Bulusan road by a motorable track.

Numerous villages lie along the park's fringes, although very few people live within the boundaries of the park itself. Furthermore, none of the Philippines' cultural minorities live in or around the Bulusan area. Several hot and cold springs have been found close to some of these villages, the most notable being Masacrot Hot Springs, on the southern edge of the park, and the Mateo Hot and Cold Springs to the west.

Fauna and Flora

Although this is a relatively small park which has seen some logging and farm encroachment, much of it is well forested, with an estimated 2,650 hectares (6,650 acres) still covered by trees. Much of the non-forested land is grassland on Mount Bulusan's upper slopes, where volcanic rock, poor soil and occasional eruptions make it impossible for trees to survive.

Some of the best forest, rich in dipterocarp trees, surrounds Lake Bulusan, although there are also areas of such forest on some of the more inaccessible slopes

Location: In Sorsogon province, in the far south of Luzon; 60 km (37 miles) south of Legaspi.

Climate: There is no clearly defined dry season, so rain can be expected at any time, although it tends to be less wet from March to May. Humidity is always high but, owing to altitude, temperatures are milder than in the lowlands; about 30°C (86°F) at Lake Bulusan and 10–15°C (50–59°F) on the summit of Mt Bulusan.

When to go: Typhoons may make it difficult to visit from June to November. March to May is likely to be the best season due to reduced rainfall.

Access: Daily flights from Manila to Legaspi. From Legaspi take a bus to Sorsogon town and then Irosin. Here hire a jeepney for the ride to San Roque or Lake Bulusan.

Permits: Obtainable at park entry points. Hikers intending to climb Mt Bulusan will be refused access if an eruption warning has been issued.

Equipment: Good walking shoes, camera, binoculars, warm clothing and full camping equipment if climbing Mt Bulusan.

Facilities: Good trail around Lake Bulusan, with viewpoint on hill above. Hiking trail to the summit of Mt Bulusan. Hot springs at Masacrot. Hot and cold springs at Mateo. Palogtok Waterfall near Masacrot.

Watching wildlife: Raptors may be seen circling overhead. Forest birds may occasionally be visible in the Lake Bulusan forest. Lizards a common sight in the forest. Excellent dipterocarp forest around Lake Bulusan.

Visitor activities: Hiking, birdwatching.

Above: *A fisherman paddles his outrigger across the waters of Lake Bulusan.*

Right: *A view across Lake Bulusan, surrounded by lowland rainforest, towards Sharp Peak, one of three mountains in the national park.*

further into the park. In addition, some areas of mossy forest exist above 1000 metres, on the slopes of Mount Bulusan and Sharp Peak.

Much of the park's animal wildlife exists in the environs of Lake Bulusan. Sixty-seven species of bird have been identified, of which 33 are Philippine endemics and five restricted to Luzon (or Luzon and its adjacent islands). The latter group consists of the Luzon Bleeding-heart Pigeon, Luzon Tarictic Hornbill, Red-crested Malkoha, Scale-feathered Malkoha and the Blackish Cuckoo-shrike. Only 11 species of mammal have so far been identified, but they include four fruit bats, the highly endangered Southern Luzon Giant Cloud Rat and the Philippine Deer. The Lake Bulusan forest area seems to be particularly rich in reptiles, as small lizards frequently scurry away from the path as hikers approach. To date 12 species have been identified.

Lake and Mountain Trails

Lake Bulusan is completely encircled by forest, and from the shore there are good views across the water to Sharp Peak. A path leads right around the lake, allowing plenty of opportunity to explore the forest and much of its life. On a hill above the southeastern shore a viewpoint has been built to allow greater appreciation of the park's mountainous interior.

Unfortunately, no paths lead away from the lakeside area into the park's interior, but for those hoping to climb Mount Bulusan a trail leads from the nearby village of San Roque. A guide is definitely needed for this climb and it will be necessary to camp at least one night on the mountain, the campsite usually being on the shore of Lake Aguingay. Note that Mount Bulusan is quite active and is occasionally closed to hikers for fear of imminent eruptions.

Right: *With several hundred species, many of them unique to the Philippines, ferns are extremely common in the rainforests, able to thrive due to the high rainfall and humidity.*

Far left: *Pandanus plants range from beachside shrubs to tall, spindly forest trees, to energetic climbers such as this one. They are extremely common in almost all Philippine lowland and montane forests, where they are easily recognized by their long, thin leaves, with edges covered in razor sharp spines.*

Left: *A skink, a very common sight on the forest floor around Lake Bulusan, scurries away when disturbed.*

MOUNT ISAROG NATIONAL PARK

A Volcano Rising from the Plains

Situated in the far south of Luzon, in the region known as Bicol, the enormous cone of Mount Isarog rises abruptly from flat, low-lying farmlands just to the east of the city of Naga, capital of Camarines Sur province. Cloaked in montane and mossy forests, the volcano was proclaimed a national park in 1938 and covers 10,100 hectares (25,000 acres). It is known for its rich wildlife, which includes several mammals unique to its slopes, and as such is one of the country's best-known protected areas.

A Sleeping Volcano

With its summit at an altitude of 1,966 metres (6,450 feet), this is the highest mountain in Camarines Sur province. Isarog sits in the middle of the Bicol Volcanic Chain, a line of six volcanoes of which three (but not Isarog itself) are active. Two craters can be found at Isarog's summit, the eastern, lower one of the

Opposite above: Mt Isarog, an inactive volcano, seen across farmland near the city of Naga, shortly after sunrise.

Opposite below left: A Philippine Hawk-eagle is a rare resident of these forests.

Opposite below right: Tradescantia growing wild along the footpath that leads down through forest towards Malabsay Falls.

Above right: Tree seedlings produced by foresters at Mt Isarog are prepared for shipment to a reforestation project.

two containing a number of fumaroles from which pours a constant cloud of steam and sulphurous gases. A number of hot springs can also be found in remote parts of the mountain's slopes.

Mount Isarog lies close to a part of the coast that is heavily indented, with the very enclosed waters of San Miguel Bay lying to the northwest and the more open Lagonoy Gulf to the east. The city of Naga lies just 17 kilometres (10 ½ miles) west of the park's main entrance at Panicuasan.

The mountain is completely surrounded by farmland, and there has been some encroachment by agriculture into the park's boundaries, as well as continued small-scale illegal logging. An estimated 4,000 people live within the park's boundaries, including a sizeable number of Agta, the local Negrito group, based mainly on Isarog's southern side, close to the town of Ocampo. Despite pressure from the surrounding population about 60 per cent of the forest cover remains intact, and thanks to local efforts reforestation programmes have been active in a number of areas.

Conservation Work and the Quest for New Species

Although there is some forest in the area around the park entrance at Panicuasan at an altitude of approximately 400 metres (1,300 feet), much of the forest is fragmented by farmland right up to 900 metres (2,950

Location: In Camarines Sur province, part of the Bicol region of the far south of Luzon. Park entrance lies 17 km (10 ½ miles) east of Naga, provincial capital.

Climate: Isarog's east and west sides have different climates. The west side has rain evenly distributed throughout the year, while the east side, facing the open sea, suffers heavy rain from November to February. Temperatures at low altitudes are usually over 30°C (86°F), but near and on the summit are often below 10°C (50°F), made worse by rain and fog.

When to go: Weather permitting, the Naga side can be visited at any time of year, but from June to October typhoons are a frequent threat.

Access: Flights several times a week from Manila to Naga; or daily flights from Manila to Legaspi, followed by a two-hour bus journey to Naga. From Naga to the park entrance ride a public jeepney to Panicuasan village, then walk 2 km (1 ¼ miles) or hire a jeepney.

Permits: If climbing to the summit, a permit must be obtained at the park office in Naga. Visitors going just to the waterfalls can obtain a permit at the Panicuasan ranger station.

Equipment: Walking shoes, rain protection, complete camping gear if climbing to the summit, leech socks, camera, binoculars.

Facilities: Paths have been cut to the waterfalls and the summit. Small clearings serve as campsites along the summit trail. The Panicuasan ranger station has a few small picnic tables. Guides are available locally.

Watching wildlife: Montane and mossy forest. Various forest birds may be visible.

Visitor activities: Hiking, bird-watching.

Above: *A mountain stream pours through dense forest near Nabuntalan Falls.*

Opposite: *Beautiful Malabsay Falls cascades through forest near the base of Mt Isarog.*

Right: *A caterpillar encountered on the forest fringes.*

feet) above sea level. Here farms finally peter out, replaced by dense, tangled stands of montane forest, which reach up to 1,500 metres (4,900 feet), where it in turn is replaced by the stunted, gnarled and moss-draped trees of the mossy forest. This forest continues all the way to Isarog's summit. To date, few studies have been conducted on the plant life, although the mossy forest especially is expected to contain a vast range of species, including pandans, rattans, orchids and vines. It is highly likely that species new to science will be found.

The first studies of the park's fauna were carried out in 1961, during which 135 species of bird were identified, giving Isarog one of the highest avian species counts of any Philippine protected area. Sadly, subsequent studies in 1988 showed that 27 of these, all lowland birds, had been wiped out in the area due to deforestation. However, the same study did identify a new species of rodent, now named the Isarog Shrew-rat, unusual not only for being unique to this mountain but also for feeding almost entirely on earthworms. In all, 45 species of mammal, four of them endemic to this mountain, have been found on Isarog, most living in the mossy forest, including the Isarog Shrew-rat. Most are bats and rodents, but there are also Philippine Warty Pigs, Philippine Deer and Long-tailed Macaques.

In 1990 Mount Isarog became one of five protected areas in the Philippines to become part of a debt-for-nature swap, in which some of the country's debts were cancelled in return for a commitment to environmental protection. During this programme Mount Isarog was administered by the Haribon Foundation, a non-government organization (NGO), which conducted some of the area's first community education and alternative livelihood programmes, aimed at helping the local people move away from environmentally destructive livelihoods. Since 1995 the park has become part of the National Integrated Protected Areas Programme (NIPAP), a scheme funded and partly managed by the European Union, designed to improve the protection of eight of the country's most important protected areas.

Exploring the Park

The main entrance to the park is via the ranger station at Panicuasan. From here one can descend a steep path into a gorge to visit the beautiful Malabsay Falls, a ribbon of water that falls into a pool and then leads off into a tumbling stream shrouded in forest greens. There is a 20-minute hike upwards to Nabuntalan Falls, another large and powerful cascade set in dense forest.

Only one summit trail open to visiting hikers exists, and this also starts from the ranger station. Initially it follows the same path towards Nabuntalan Falls, but then continues steeply upwards through a mixture of farmland and secondary forest until the upper montane forest is reached. There then follows a tiring, and usually damp, scramble through the mossy forest to the summit craters. Allow for at least one night's stay on the mountain and be sure to take a guide: there are several campsites along the way, all known to the guides.

MINDORO

Mindoro is a wild and rugged island, sparsely populated and relatively undeveloped. Its northern tip is just 130 kilometres (80 miles) south of Manila, and yet this is a wholly different world, far removed from the big city's hustle and bustle, its traffic jams and cellular phones.

The majority of Mindoro's population lives along the coasts, the interior consisting of a spine of high mountains that runs along the island's length. The highest peaks are Mount Halcon (2,587 metres/8,488 feet) and Mount Baco (2,487 metres/8,160 feet), both foci for important wild areas. The few people inhabiting the interior belong to the indigenous Mangyan group, a cultural minority thought to number about 30,000. Whilst they have a very well-established culture and lore that gives the group a clear identity in which many take pride, most are extremely poor.

Although the island is wild, it is not pristine. Through much of this century its once dense forests have been rapidly cleared, to the point that today only isolated pockets remain. This is a serious situation since Mindoro is one of the Philippines' five major faunal regions, complete with its own unique wildlife. The most famous of these is the Tamaraw, a dwarf buffalo, which today survives only in a few remote areas. There are also six endemic bird species, three of which face extinction. To protect what remains, some of the forest has been incorporated into Mounts Iglit-Baco National Park, although there are also numerous other forests, one of the more accessible of which is the Sablayan Watershed Forest, close to the west coast. Mount Halcon, although unprotected, remains one of the largest and wildest areas of forest surviving on Mindoro.

Around the coasts are some of the country's most spectacular coral reefs. The most easily visited are those at Puerto Galera, in the far north of the island, while one of the country's largest atoll reef complexes is found at Apo Reef Marine Natural Park, 30 kilometres (19 miles) off Mindoro's west coast.

MOUNT HALCON

A Mountain Wilderness

Location: In the northern part of Oriental Mindoro province, approx. 20 km (12 miles) southwest of Calapan, the provincial capital.

With an altitude of 2,587 metres (8,488 feet), this is Mindoro's highest mountain. It is also one of the wildest and most rugged areas in an already wild and rugged island, home to one of the largest remaining tracts of forest in Mindoro. Although officially designated a protected area, there is presently no conservation management here and park boundaries are meaningless.

Rugged Terrain and a Unique Environment

This huge mountain rears up dramatically from the coastal plain of eastern Mindoro, southwest of the town of Calapan. Not of volcanic origin, Halcon was created by massive up-lifting millions of years ago, and is believed to be a fragment of the Southeast Asian landmass. As a result, Halcon has geological similarities with Mount Kinabalu in Malaysia's Sabah, and a flora that is transitional between those of Borneo and Palawan on the one hand and the bulk of the Philippines on the other.

The uniqueness of Halcon's environment is further enhanced by the sheer volume of rain. Being on Mindoro's east coast, there is no distinct dry season, and heavy rain is virtually a daily occurrence. This guarantees an enormous fecundity of life, particularly in the mossy forest areas above about 1,400 metres (4,600 feet). Here, the trees are dense and gnarled, adorned with thick layers of dripping moss, orchids, ferns, pitcher plants and other vines and epiphytes. Everywhere there is water, in standing pools or rushing down the mountain in clear, fast-moving streams. There are 21 major waterfalls on the mountain, all still unnamed, six of the most spectacular – huge ribbons of water pouring vertically down the mountainside – visible in one view of the mountain's upper slopes. This is a wild, primeval landscape, a place where nature is still firmly in control.

On such a large mountain it ought to be possible to see a wide range of habitats, from lowland dipterocarp forests, through montane forests, to mossy forest and finally grasslands around the peaks. Unfortunately, clearance for agriculture has removed all the accessible dipterocarp forest, and by the time the fields give way to trees the habitat has already changed to montane forest.

Climate: Extremely wet. Rain falls on most days throughout the year, though April–May has the least rain. Temperatures on the lower slopes are usually over 30°C (86°F). At Camp One it is often only 10°C (50°F), especially during rain, and at the summit rain may bring the temperature down to only 5–6°C (41–43°F).

When to go: April–May is the best time. Do not climb during the typhoon season (June –November) as these storms cause severe conditions on the mountain.

Access: Bus from Manila to Batangas, then high-speed catamaran ferry to Calapan. Hire a vehicle to go from Calapan to Lantuyang.

Permits: Permit available from Halcon Mountaineers in Calapan. In addition, an entry fee is payable to the *barangay* captain (village chief) at Lantuyang.

Equipment: Full hiking and camping gear; waterproof clothing and covers for rucksacks; all food must be carried in; good hiking boots; insect repellent; leech socks; binoculars, camera.

Facilities: Excellent guides available from Halcon Mountaineers. They maintain direct radio link to Base Camp in Calapan throughout the hike. Cleared areas inside the forest form the only camping sites. Plenty of watercourses in the forest provide clean drinking water. Accommodation available in Calapan.

Watching wildlife: A massive profusion of plant life to be seen. Animal wildlife, except leeches, difficult to see.

Visitor activities: Hiking, photography.

Opposite above: The summit of Mt Halcon, seen from a forest clearing at Camp One.

Opposite Below: Fording a stream on the lower slopes of Mt Halcon, when still in open countryside.

Above right: The starting point for any climb up Mt Halcon is the headquarters of Halcon Mountaineers, in Calapan.

Previous pages:

Page 56: *A view of the Puerto Galera coastline, seen from the slopes of Mt Malasimbo. Page 57: The Asian Glossy Starling is a common bird in both farmland and woodland.*

To Batangas

Escarceo Point
Puerto Galera
Verde Island Passage
Dulangan River
San Teodoro
Calapan — Calapan Point
Base Camp
Silonay
Manila
Mindoro
Baco
Naujan
Lagarinan Point
Mt Dulangan
Malaysia
MINDORO
Lumangbayan
Mt Halcon
2587m
(8488ft)
Bungao
Mount Halcon
Victoria
Naujan Lake
Tigbao
Pola

Right: *Flowering* Medinilla, *a shrub of mid-montane forests, makes a striking show of colour amid the dense greens.*

Far right: *Pitcher plants can sometimes be seen in the mossy forest, particularly where the soil is very poor.*

Below: *Trees in the montane forest are festooned with hundreds of orchids, many of which produce tiny flowers that can be easily overlooked in the dense vegetation.*

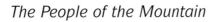

Here the trees are still tall and straight, but much smaller than in a dipterocarp forest, and many are festooned with climbing bamboos and at higher altitudes an increasing number of epiphytes, especially orchids and ferns. At approximately 1,400 metres (4,600 feet) the upper montane forest gives way to the dank, fecund environment of the mossy forest, which stretches up to an altitude of approximately 2,000 metres (6,500 feet). From here, trees give way to grassland, which reaches all the way to the summit.

The People of the Mountain

There are several villages of Mindoro's indigenous people, the Mangyan, on Halcon's lower slopes, amounting to a population of several hundred people. The Mangyan, who are spread right across the island, are subdivided into seven major groups, those living here belonging to the Alangan.

Almost all extremely poor, for the most part they play little role in the mainstream economy, subsisting instead as slash-and-burn hill farmers. Although not the cause of the massive deforestation that has ripped through their island in the past 50 years, today their insistence on adhering to slash-and-burn farming methods threatens those wild environments that do remain, including Mount Halcon.

Climbing the Mountain

Mount Halcon is undoubtedly the Philippines' ultimate mountaineering challenge, despite not being the country's highest mountain. This is partly because the hike starts barely 50 metres (160 feet) above sea level. Moreover, the path does not go straight up but instead has first to climb Mount Dulangan, a 1,500 metre (4,900 feet) hill that bars the way to Halcon. From the summit of Dulangan the trail drops down to the Dulangan River at an altitude of 500 metres (1,600 feet) before once again climbing all the way to Halcon's summit. This makes for a massive 4,580 metre (15,027 feet) climb, leaving this a bigger haul than that to the summit of Mount Everest from its base camp!

The starting point is Base Camp, the office and shop of Halcon Mountaineers, an enthusiastic and skilled band of climbers, in Calapan. They will organize and guide your hike, an essential team for a venture into this truly wild area. The hiking starts at the little Mangyan

settlement of Lantuyang, from where there is a three-hour climb across fields before one finally enters the forest. After several hours of walking through montane and then mossy forest, the summit of Mount Dulangan is reached, after which the trail immediately starts to descend. After dropping 100 metres (330 feet) Camp One is reached, one of two possible sites for the first night's camp. It is located in an area from which the forest has been partially cleared by lightning strikes followed by erosion. The result is a specialized flora, including hundreds of tiny sundew plants, as well as stupendous views of Halcon's summit and huge waterfalls cascading down the upper slopes.

From Camp One the path drops very steeply to the Dulangan River, on the banks of which is Camp Two, another possible site for the first night's camp. The river needs to be forded and then from here the path climbs steeply towards the summit, for 1,000 metres (3,300 feet) squeezing through dense mossy forest but eventually striking out across rough, open grassland. Some of the higher parts are very steep, one section having to be negotiated with a ladder, before the path makes its way across the aptly named Knife Edge. Finally, the summit is reached, and tired hikers are rewarded on clear days with incredible views across much of Mindoro.

Above: *Mt Halcon's mossy forest is a primeval place of tangled trees, hanging, dripping wet moss, and plenty of running water.*

PUERTO GALERA MARINE RESERVE

A Well-protected Submarine World

Puerto Galera is a well-known and beautiful beach resort area lying at the northern tip of Mindoro, about 130 kilometres (80 miles) south of Manila. Not only is it blessed with an almost uncountable number of beaches scattered among its many islands and bays, but beneath the waves are to be found some of the country's most stunning coral reefs. It is not surprising that this has become one of the Philippines' most popular attractions, with both overseas visitors and Filipinos coming to enjoy the beautiful scenery, both above and below the water.

UNESCO Protection for the Reefs

So extensive and diverse are these reefs that they have been the centre of scientific study for a good many years, the University of the Philippines establishing a marine

studies centre here as far back as 1934. Almost half a century later, in 1973, the United Nations Education, Science and Cultural Organization (UNESCO) named Puerto Galera's reefs a Man and the Biosphere Marine Reserve. At the same time, the area's forested mountainous hinterland, principally Mounts Malasimbo and Talipanan, were also named a Man and the Biosphere Reserve, thus highlighting the whole Puerto Galera area as a valuable marine and terrestrial environment of global importance.

Whilst the protection given to the terrestrial areas has been less successful, the marine reserve has been well looked after, ensuring that today most of Puerto Galera's reefs are in excellent condition, providing a rich diversity of marine life and, as a result, some of the best diving and snorkelling in the country. Although the university's marine studies centre closed down some time ago research still continues, scientists travelling down from Manila for occasional surveys. The reefs remain protected not through any government protected-area programme but owing to the efforts of local people, fishermen, hotel owners and dive operators cooperating to try to ensure that all parts of the local economy benefit from the undersea riches.

A Popular Resort

The area as a whole focuses on the small town of Puerto Galera, situated at the innermost point of Muelle Bay, a beautiful natural harbour almost completely enclosed by a peninsula to the east and a cluster of islands, Boquete

Opposite far left above: Feeding fish is a popular activity for divers, though one that should not be recommended.

Opposite far left middle: Tubastraea cup corals, with their tentacles protruding as they 'hunt' for food in the current.

Opposite far left below: A Moray Eel makes a foray from a crevass in the reef.

Opposite left: A barrel sponge surrounded by clusters of hard and soft corals, a very typical view of Puerto Galera's coral reefs.

Above right: Big La Laguna Beach is one of the most attractive and popular of Puerto Galera's beaches.

Location: In Oriental Mindoro province, at the northern tip of Mindoro, about 130 km (80 miles) south of Manila.

Climate: There is no distinct dry season, with rain likely at any time of the year. However, April–May is usually the driest period. Temperatures are usually over 30°C (86°F), although sea breezes can make night times quite cool, especially in January. Humidity is always high, usually about 80%.

When to go: It is possible to dive on the reefs at any time of year, although March–October is thought to be the best period.

Access: Bus from Manila to Batangas (three hours), and then a ferry to Puerto Galera (1–2 hours depending on type of ferry). Take a boat, tricycle or jeepney from the Puerto Galera wharf to the beach of choice.

Permits: Not needed.

Equipment: Swimming costume, sunglasses, sunblock, camera. All diving and snorkelling equipment can be hired, but divers can bring their own if they prefer.

Facilities: Plenty of accommodation at the beaches. Most dive operators are based at Sabang and Big and Small La Laguna Beaches, though there are also a few at White Beach. Most run a range of diving courses from novice to instructor level. Plenty of boats for hire, for diving, snorkelling, swimming or just touring.

Watching wildlife: The underwater world teems with life, from a vast array of corals to a diversity of fish. Butterflyfish, Moorish Idols, sweetlips and soldierfish are all common. Huge barrel sponges are found at some of the dive sites.

Visitor activities: Exploring the beaches by boat or foot; swimming; snorkelling; diving.

Above: *A dive boat moored close to the shore at Big La Laguna Beach.*

Right: *A Linckia starfish, a very common inhabitant of Puerto Galera's reefs.*

and San Antonio, to the west. Arriving here by ferry from Luzon is a memorable experience, as the ship sails past a series of headlands into the hidden Muelle Bay, a sparkling aquamarine expanse of water surrounded by low hills stunningly green in their cloak of coconut palms. Brilliant white yachts lie at anchor scattered across the innermost parts of the bay, while in the background looms Mount Malasimbo, a brooding deep green, invariably covered in a heavy blanket of cloud.

On arrival at the wharf one is hardly aware of the town – just a few roofs visible through coconut palms and a line of small shops and cafes along the waterfront giving its presence away. In any case, few visitors stay in the town long, almost all being whisked away by boat or vehicle to any one of the beaches that lie to the east and west. Those intent on exploring the coral reefs usually head eastwards to the beaches of Big and Small La Laguna or Sabang, lying at the outermost

end of the Puerto Galera peninsula, though there are also beaches to the west, such as White Beach, where there is some diving available.

Diving on the Coral Reefs

Most of the coral reefs lie off the northern coastline of the peninsula, within easy reach of some of the main beaches. The submarine terrain varies from gently sloping and shallow coral gardens with a sandy floor, to steep rocky drop-offs or vertical walls descending into deep water. Moreover, with the coastline consisting of so many islands, inlets and headlands, the degree of exposure varies enormously from place to place, leaving some reefs in calm, sheltered waters, and others exposed to the open sea and strong tidal currents.

The result of such varied terrain and exposure is a great diversity of marine life, ranging from large expanses of hard corals in the shallow areas, such as Acropora table and staghorn corals, populated with shoals of tiny reef fish such as soldierfish, sergeant majors and butterflyfish, to large Gorgonian sea-fans, *Tubastraea* cup corals and barrel sponges in the deeper.

deeper, more exposed places where currents often run fast and fierce. Here shoals of larger reef fish are found, such as triggerfish, parrotfish, wrasse and sweetlips, as well as deep water pelagics, including barracuda, tuna and occasionally sharks, mostly Whitetip Reef Sharks. Moray Eels lurk in the crevasses found on many of the rocky slopes and walls, while rays are common in the sandy areas. Everywhere, soft corals are abundant, including delicately branching and often vividly coloured soft tree corals, large and lobed mushroom leather corals and the delicately 'leaved' palm corals.

A string of dive sites has become well established, covering all these habitats and conditions, those close inshore and in shallow, sheltered waters benefiting the novice diver and snorkeller, those further out in the exposed waters of Verde Island Passage appealing to divers with more experience. Many of the dive sites' names reflect local conditions or the dive's main high-light, from such mild places as Coral Garden or Sweetlips Cave to the rougher sites that include The Canyons, Shark Cave or The Washing Machine, the last of these so named for the violence of its currents!

Above: *A trio of Moorish Idols swim past clusters of coral.*

Below: *The hard, brittle spikes of an* Acropora *hard coral, widespread across the reefs in shallower water.*

MOUNT MALASIMBO

A Man and the Biosphere Reserve

Located at the northernmost tip of Mindoro, Mount Malasimbo is the highest of a line of three mountains that form a dramatic, and still largely forested, backdrop to the stunningly beautiful resort area of Puerto Galera. Just 130 kilometres (80 miles) south of Manila, the region is readily accessible by bus and ferry and has plenty of accommodation to offer.

A UNESCO-Recognized Protected Area

With its magnificent coastline, dense rainforests and vibrant submarine coral reefs making for a highly varied and species-rich environment, back in 1973 the United Nations Education, Science and Cultural Organization (UNESCO) made the whole of Puerto Galera, including Mount Malasimbo and the offshore coral reefs, a Man and the Biosphere Reserve. This is an accolade awarded to what the organization considers to be natural environments of global conservation and biodiversity importance.

Opposite above: *The dome of Mt Talipanan, adjacent to Mt Malasimbo, and more visible from White Beach.*

Opposite below: *White Beach, in the east of Puerto Galera, is the most convenient accommodation area close to Mt Malasimbo.*

Above right: *Butterflies are common around flowering forest shrubs, or beside streams where salts are available.*

The three mountains, Mount Malasimbo (1,228 metres/4,029 feet), Mount Talipanan (1,185 metres/3,888 feet) and the smaller Mount Alinbayan, make up the bulk of the terrestrial component of the reserve, forming a chain almost 12 kilometres (7½ miles) long, running parallel to the coast and with just a narrow coastal plain between the shore and their lower slopes. Although their reserve status since 1973 has not ensured protection, resulting over the years in an increasing human presence and the encroachment and conversion of the mountains' lower slopes to farmland, many areas are still well forested. The upper slopes of Mount Malasimbo, for example, are still well covered with mossy forest, while lower areas of all three have montane forest and – albeit rather patchy – stands of lowland dipterocarp forest, especially Lauan, or Philippine Mahogany.

Birdlife is still extensive even in the areas of disturbed forest and, despite the present lack of any clear programme of conservation management for these mountains, ornithologists from the University of the Philippines make regular surveys to assess the bird populations.

The People of the Mountain

The mountains' lower slopes are home to several villages of Mangyan people, Mindoro's original inhabitants.

Map labels:
Verde Island Passage
Long Beach
San Antonio
Big La Laguna Beach
Small La Laguna Beach
Sabang
Sinandigan
Boquete
Minola Bay
Muelle Bay
Minola
Balatero
San Isidro
White Beach
PUERTO GALERA PENINSULA
Aninuan
Aninuan Falls
Puerto Galera
Hundura Beach
Ponderosa Golf and Country Club
Varadero Bay
Talipanan Falls
Tamaraw Falls
Dulangan Beach
Dulangan
▲ Mt Talipanan
Villaflor
▲ Mt Malasimbo
Mount Malasimbo
Manila
Mindoro
Malaysia

Location: At the northern tip of Mindoro, 130 km (80 miles) south of Manila, in Oriental Mindoro province.

Climate: No clear-cut dry season, with the possibility of rain at any time of the year. Temperatures generally around 35–36°C (95–96°F) during April–May, and about 30°C (86°F) in January and February.

When to go: The area can be visited at any time, but rain can be expected throughout the year. April–May is likely to be the driest period.

Access: From Manila by bus to Batangas and then by ferry to Puerto Galera. Bus journey time is about three hours. Ferries take 1–2 hours, depending on type. From southern Mindoro, head for Calapan and then travel by jeepney to Puerto Galera. From Occidental Mindoro take a ferry from Sablayan or Abra de Ilog to Batangas and then another ferry back to Puerto Galera.

Permits: Not needed, but a guide should be taken for forest hikes.

Equipment: Walking shoes, hat, sunblock, water, snacks, camera, binoculars.

Facilities: Farm trails through the forests. Motorable track up to the Ponderosa Golf and Country Club. Plenty of accommodation at the beach resorts, the nearest of which is White Beach.

Watching wildlife: A variety of bird life, plus dipterocarp and montane forest trees. Below the canopy are palms, pandanus, rattans and various flowers.

Visitor activities: Hiking, birdwatching, photography.

associated with coastal tourism, that has caused the fragmentation of Malasimbo's forest. In addition, there is also some small-scale mining and quarrying, the latter mainly for marble, which have eaten into the forest.

Exploring the Forest

Although the mossy forest areas on the upper slopes of Mount Malasimbo have few if any paths through them, being penetrable only by skilled Mangyan hunters, the lower forests are criss-crossed by a network of paths. One of the best places to visit simply for a good view of the forest is the Ponderosa Golf and Country Club, a one-time cattle ranch now converted into what must be one of the world's steepest golf courses, set on Malasimbo's middle slopes.

Anyone intending to hike in the forest should hire guides, preferably a lowland Filipino who can speak English and a Mangyan who almost certainly will know the forest well. The patchiness of the forest ensures superb views across Puerto Galera and the sea beyond, while within the forest there is the usual dense vegetation to investigate, although all of it easily navigated via the well-used paths. There are also a number of waterfalls to head for, one of the remotest being Talipanan Falls, a cascade tumbling down a rocky slope, surrounded by forest and set at the very foot of the towering Mount Talipanan. Other waterfalls include Aninuan Falls, close to the coastal village of Aninuan and accessible without the need for a guide. To the south of Puerto Galera, close to the main road towards Calapan are Tamaraw Falls, probably the largest of the area's waterfalls.

Above: *Talipanan Falls lies in an area of lowland rainforest, on the slopes of Mt Talipanan.*

Right: *Olive-backed Sunbirds are a common sight in flowering trees both in parks and forests.*

About 30,000 Mangyan live throughout Mindoro, divided into seven major groups, with those around Puerto Galera belonging almost entirely to the Iraya group. They are still a largely primitive group of people, with little role in the mainstream Philippine economy. They are almost invariably very poor, subsisting through slash-and-burn farming, a practice that many of the Mangyan elders insist on maintaining as an inherent part of their tradition, despite the extensive damage caused to Mindoro's natural environment.

It is partly the Mangyan's slash-and-burn farming, combined with conversion of some areas to coconut plantations and the spread of property development

SABLAYAN WATERSHED FOREST RESERVE

A Lake Surrounded by Lowland Rainforest

This is one of Mindoro's few remaining and most accessible areas of lowland rainforest. About 25 kilometres (16 miles) southeast of Sablayan, a small town half-way down Mindoro's west coast, this forest is quite unique in being an integral part of the sprawling Sablayan Penal Colony. This factor alone has probably ensured its survival, yet despite the unusual nature of the area's residents visitors are welcome.

A Green Refuge

Set in rolling countryside just east of the main west coast road, the penal colony is a sprawling prison largely without bars. The prison itself is a small walled compound, but it stands surrounded by a mixture of agricultural land and forest, all of it part of the colony, the fields and much of the infrastructure worked by inmates. Within the landscape are scattered, tidy villages, where staff, inmates' relatives and ex-inmates live.

Beyond the last of the villages the motorable track comes to an end at the edge of the forest and beside one of the area's most attractive features, Lake Libao. The shore of this lake is the starting point for any visit to the Sablayan Forest. Thought to be of volcanic origin, this essentially circular lake is quite shallow, allowing its surface to be scattered with water lilies and small

Above right: The bukas-bukas flower is common around the forest fringes and in clearings. The local people claim it has medicinal properties, and is used to treat skin ailments.

islands. As a result, it is alive with birds, including kingfishers, egrets, bitterns, Purple Herons and Philippine Mallards. This is an excellent location for wading birds. Several more similar lakes lie hidden in the surrounding hills – Libao is simply the most accessible.

Forested hills enclose the lake on three sides, and although much of the forest is badly disturbed it is still dense and for the most part quite impenetrable. Birdlife readily seen here includes the Emerald Ground Dove, the Mindoro Bleeding-heart Pigeon and the Black-hooded Coucal (both the latter being highly threatened birds endemic to the island). There are several colonies of fruit bats, and it is claimed that at least one part of the forest visible from the lake still harbours a reasonably healthy number of Tamaraw, the highly endangered dwarf buffalo unique to Mindoro.

Conservation in the Sablayan Forest

The Sablayan Watershed Forest is perhaps the most important segment of lowland rainforest of those that lie scattered along Mindoro's west coast. Survivors of the island's once extensive rainforests, these small areas are vital to the protection of Mindoro's wildlife, most especially the Tamaraw, yet most are not within any officially protected area. The Sablayan forest probably receives more protection than most owing to its position inside the penal colony.

Map labels: To Mamburao; Buenavista; Sablayan; Manila; Mindoro; Malaysia; LUZON SEA; Sablayan Watershed Forest; Dongo Point; Lake Libao; Sablayan Penal Colony; N; Pianag; To San José

Location: In Occidental Mindoro province, about 25 km (16 miles) southeast of Sablayan, a few kilometres east of the Sablayan–San José main road.

Climate: Dry from November or December to May, raining from June to October or November. Temperatures are often 35–36°C (95–96°F) during April–May, when humidity is also high, and about 30°C (86°F) in January. Temperatures may be below 30°C (86°F) during the rainy season.

When to go: January and February are the driest and coolest months, making this a good time for walking. March–May is also dry but increasingly hot.

Access: By air from Manila to San José followed by a bus journey to Sablayan, or by bus from Manila to Batangas and then overnight ferry from Batangas to Sablayan. From Sablayan either hire a vehicle to take you all the way to the lake, or take a bus bound for San José as far as the turn-off to the penal colony, and then walk.

Permits: Not needed, but register with the guard at the penal colony's main gate. You may be asked to visit the colony's superintendent en route to the lake.

Equipment: Walking shoes, hat, binoculars, camera, snacks and water.

Facilities: Footpath around lake, but no sign-posting. Accommodation planned for the lakeside, but as yet not built.

Watching wildlife: Wading birds, especially Purple Herons and egrets. Also Philippine Mallards, kingfishers and Mindoro Bleeding-heart Pigeons. Chances of seeing a Tamaraw are slim.

Visitor activities: Walking, birdwatching, photography.

Above: *The lily-covered waters of Lake Libao, surrounded by lowland rainforest.*

Right: *The Bog Bean is a common plant, growing in the lake's shallow margins.*

In the early 1990s it was planned that these forest areas, including Sablayan, would be included in a new priority protected area, one of the World Bank-funded components of the Integrated Protected Areas System (IPAS). Unfortunately, this plan was dropped owing to opposition from the Mangyan people, suspicious of outside government interference in their lives. More recently, however, they have become part of the European Union-funded National Integrated Protected Areas Programme (NIPAP), and are now becoming the focus of conservation measures designed to run alongside measures intended for Mounts Iglit-Baco National Park, at 75,500 hectares (186,500 acres) Mindoro's largest protected area, sprawling across the highlands of southern Mindoro.

Exploring the Lake and Forest

While a penal colony may not seem the most likely place to be open to outsiders, visitors are in fact welcome. To reach Lake Libao and the forest from the main road it is necessary to walk or drive right across the colony, first registering at the main entrance. The main track eventually leads to the lakeside, where a beautiful view,

Left: *A tangle of vegetation, with a mass of fruiting bodies hanging down from a palm inside Sablayan's lowland forest.*

Above: *An array of colourful beetles, many of them hardly studied, can be seen lurking among the forest floor vegetation.*

complete with covered viewing area, welcomes the visitor. Drinks and snacks may be available here from inmates, distinguishable from the guards only by the colour of their T-shirts and the fact that they are not armed!

To explore the area, follow the footpath that goes right around the lake. Scrubby vegetation on the lake's edge often gives good cover, allowing quite close views of the lake's birdlife, especially of Purple Herons sitting on the lake's islets. Once on the far side of the lake, it may be possible to penetrate some way into the forest, but it is very dense and the footpaths are few and far between; take care not to get lost in the tangle of vegetation.

Left: *Local men fishing in the shallows of the lake.*

APO REEF MARINE NATURAL PARK

A Deep-sea Atoll Reef

This vast reef complex, lying about 30 kilometres (19 miles) off the west coast of Mindoro, is one of the Philippines' largest coral reefs and one of its few atoll structures. Initially designated a marine park in 1978, Apo Reef is of great importance to both local fisheries and conservation, as well as being a popular location for visiting divers. Since the mid-1990s it has been one of the country's 10 priority protected sites, as one of the World Bank-funded components of the Integrated Protected Areas System (IPAS).

A Remote Submarine World

Covering an area 26 kilometres (16 miles) from north to south and 20 kilometres (12 miles) east to west, all but 29

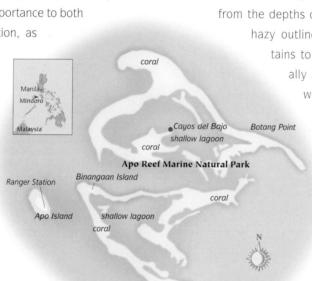

coral

Manila
Mindoro

Malaysia

coral

Cayos del Bajo
shallow lagoon

Botang Point

Apo Reef Marine Natural Park

Ranger Station

Binangaan Island

coral

Apo Island

shallow lagoon

coral

N

coral

hectares (72 acres) of the reef's total 15,800 hectares (39,000 acres) is below water, making Apo a hidden treasure. Only paler shades of blue water give away the locations of shallow areas, reef 'mountains' rearing up from the depths of the sea. Apart from the hazy outlines of the Mindoro mountains to the east, these are virtually the only 'landmarks' by which the reef can be identified. It lies almost in the centre of the Mindoro Strait, a mostly very deep stretch of water that separates Mindoro to the east from the Calamian Islands, the northernmost part of Palawan, to the southwest.

The reef consists of two atolls, one to the north and one to the south, both more or less triangular in shape, separated by a 30 metre (100 feet) deep channel. Corals delineate the edges of each atoll, dropping away steeply into deep water all around. Within this coral barrier each atoll contains a lagoon of very shallow water (about two metres/six feet deep) characterized by a beautiful white sandy bottom.

Only in three places does the coral rise above the sea's surface, creating the islands of Cayos de Bajo, Binangaan and Apo. The first of these is a 250–300 square metre (2,700–3,250 square feet) flat islet lying in the northern atoll, while the second is an outcrop of jagged coralline limestone on the northwestern tip of the southern atoll. Apo Island is the largest piece of land, and lies about one kilometre (600 yards) west of the

Opposite far left above: Pufferfish are a common sight, usually lurking half-hidden in reef crevasses.

Opposite far left middle: Detail of a Dendronephthya soft tree coral, common and extremely colourful residents of many parts of the reef.

Opposite far left below: A nudibranch, a highly varied and colourful group of marine slugs, crawls across the reef.

Opposite left: A dive boat makes its way across the shallows of Apo Reef, a scene of gloriously clear aquamarine and turquoise tropical water.

Above right: A male Green Turtle, a common sight for divers on Apo Reef.

Above: *A dusk view of the sandy shoreline, backed by mangrove trees, on Apo Island.*

Right: *Outcrops of coralline limestone line the shore at the southwestern end of Apo Island, with mangroves a short distance behind.*

western tip of the southern atoll, the two separated from each other by a deep channel. The island covers an area of 22 hectares (54 acres), although only 11 hectares (27 acres) can be said to be dry land. The remainder consists of mangroves, which stretch along most of the island's western, exposed, coast, as well as a small lagoon that lies sheltered within the mangroves.

The Undersea World

This vast reef, consisting of a great range of submarine habitats, from shallow sandy areas characterized by only scattered coral heads, through coral reef flats and reef crests around the edges of the lagoons, to steep or near-vertical drop-offs into the oceanic depths, is rich in marine life. Most of the Philippines' 450 species of coral can be found here, from tiny bubble corals to huge Gorgonian sea-fans, the former growing in almost any sheltered corner, the latter standing proud on the steep walls, open to the fierce currents that sweep food through their branching 'fronds'. Other invertebrates are common too, including the enormous barrel sponge, tiny sea-squirts and vibrantly colourful feather starfish.

. The diversity of fish is similarly wide, from small reef fish, such as Moorish Idols, to the larger deep-sea fish such as barracuda or tuna. Sharks can sometimes be seen too, including Hammerheads, and turtles – both Green and Hawksbill – are common.

On Apo Island, the tracks of nesting turtles can sometimes be seen on the beaches that fringe the eastern and southern shores, while the mangroves are home to an array of birds, including Pied Imperial Pigeons and Black-naped Orioles. The endangered Nicobar Pigeon has been sighted here too, although none has been spotted for a number of years now.

Conservation

Apo Reef was declared a marine park in 1978 because of its great beauty, tourism potential and importance in biodiversity and fisheries. Despite being a protected

area, since then it has been damaged by over-fishing and the use of dynamite and cyanide. Nevertheless, it remains a vital fisheries resource, and in terms of wildlife conservation is still of great importance to nesting marine turtles. For divers, the reef remains a major attraction, as many areas of the reef are still in excellent condition, with good and highly varied coral cover, as well as extensive fish life.

Since the mid-1990s, Apo Reef has been incorporated into the new IPAS, and for this reason has been renamed Apo Reef Marine Natural Park. In the past, the major problem for park rangers was the difficulty of policing such a vast and remote area of sea, but with new funding a permanent ranger station, equipped with radios and boats, has been established on Apo Island, something that has already greatly improved

Left: *A diver lines himself up to take a photograph of a well-placed feather star.*

Below: *The polyps of this* Heliofungia *mushroom coral are easily confused with those of a sea anemone.*

Bottom: *A coral slope, covered in an exuberant mixture of hard and soft corals, an array of reef fish making this their home.*

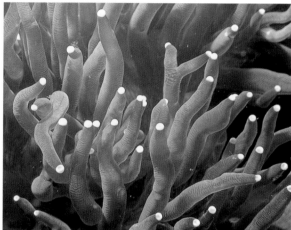

the protection given to the reef – in particular those areas close to the island.

Diving on the Reef

Access to Apo Island is restricted, but divers are allowed to dive more or less where they choose on the reef. The reef can reliably be reached only during the calm period of March to May, requiring a boat ride of a couple of hours even from Sablayan, the nearest town on Mindoro. Most dive boats head for an area on the outer northern edge of the reef, as well as the western edge of the southern atoll, close to Apo Island. These sites give divers a chance to see the full diversity of Apo's submarine habitats and hence marine life. Sightings of turtles are common, and sharks are encountered from time to time.

Right: *A beautiful butterflyfish, of which there are many species, a common resident of any Philippine coral reef.*

Below: *Spinifex grasses, more normally recognized as an Australian plant, mark the boundary between scrub and beach.*

WESTERN AND CENTRAL VISAYAS

This large archipelago, consisting of Panay, Guimaras, Negros, Cebu, Masbate and the Romblon Islands (namely Romblon itself, Tablas and Sibuyan), makes up the larger part of the Visayan region, which represents the fractured mass of islands that constitutes the central-western region of the Philippines.

Based on the land linkages that existed among these islands during the last Ice Age, about 18,000 years ago, a time when sea levels were 120 metres (394 feet) lower than today, almost the whole of this region belongs to a single major biogeographic zone, the Greater Negros-Panay Faunal Region. Only the Romblon Islands remain distinct.

Among the Romblon Islands, only Sibuyan is still of major importance to biodiversity. A beautiful island dominated by Mount Guiting Guiting, much of its natural environment, from coral reefs offshore to mossy forest and grassland around the mountain's peaks, is intact. Existing within its own biogeographic zone, Sibuyan's fauna and flora are related to those of Luzon, Mindoro and the Visayas and yet are also distinct, having several unique species of mammal.

Within the Greater Negros-Panay region high population pressure and a plantation economy have greatly reduced the forested areas. Some of the most important that remain are on Negros, such as Mount Kanlaon and the Northern Negros Forest Reserve, home to such endangered Visayan endemic wildlife as the Visayan Warty Pig and Visayan Spotted Deer. On Cebu few natural forests remain, but off its east coast an area of mudflats and mangroves on Olango Island is the country's most important site for migratory wetland birds.

77

SIBUYAN ISLAND & MOUNT GUITING GUITING NATURAL PARK

An Island Wilderness

Situated in the north of the Visayas, the rather isolated island of Sibuyan has one of the most intact natural environments in the entire country. This ranges from coral reefs offshore through beach and mangrove forests along the shoreline, to lowland, montane and mossy forests as one travels inland and climbs ever higher up the slopes of Mount Guiting Guiting, a huge mountain that dominates the island's landscape. Only recently recognized as critical to the conservation of Philippine biodiversity, Sibuyan's mountainous interior was declared a natural park in 1996 and is now part of the European Union-funded National Integrated Protected Areas Programme (NIPAP).

Opposite: The clear waters of the Cantingas River pour away from the southern slopes of Mt Guiting Guiting.

Above right: The Blue-naped Parrot occurs in lowland forest and at forest edges, nesting in the cavities of large trees and feeding on fruit.

Previous pages:
Page 78: *The densely forested Mt Guiting Guiting, fronted by mangroves along a river close to the town of Magdiwang, on the north coast of Sibuyan Island.*
Page 79: *A collection of soft tree corals, translucent and delicately branched, common but very small members of Philippine reefs.*

A Magnificent Emerald Isle

Covering an area of 450 square kilometres (180 square miles), the island is dominated by Mount Guiting Guiting, which rises directly from the coastal plain to a height of 2,050 metres (6,725 feet). From its lowest slopes up to Mayo's Peak, a secondary summit at 1,550 metres (5,000 feet), the mountain is covered in primary forest, although from this point up to the main summit the rugged terrain consists only of grass and bare rock. From Mayo's Peak down to approximately 1,350 metres (4,400 feet) the steep slopes are cloaked in mossy forest, a region of stunted trees draped in ferns, orchids and moss, while below this – down to approximately 650 metres (2,100 feet) – is montane forest, characterized by much taller, straighter trees, draped in vines and climbing bamboo, and interspersed with pandanus plants, rattans and tree ferns. Below 650 metres (2,100 feet) is lowland rainforest, the land of the giant dipterocarp trees.

Originally the lowland forest stretched right across the narrow coastal plain that encircles Mount Guiting Guiting, but extensive logging from the 1940s until 1992 cleared almost all of this, although patches still survive on the mountain's lower slopes. In some parts of the coastal plain the lowland forest has started to regenerate, to the point that secondary forest now reaches all the way to the shore, merging with extensive mangroves.

Location: In the Sibuyan Sea, about 75 km (47 miles) northeast of Panay and 60 km (37 miles) west of Masbate.

Climate: Rain is spread throughout the year, though most falls from July to December. April and May are the driest, hottest times. Daytime temperatures in the lowlands range from 28°C (82°F) in January to 34°C (93°F) in May. In the mountains the temperature quickly drops with altitude, falling to about 10°C (50°F), or lower when wet, at the summit.

When to go: Climb Guiting Guiting in April or May, when rainfall is at its lowest. For exploring the lowlands, any time from January to May offers reasonable weather.

Access: From Manila, travel by bus to Batangas and then catch a ferry, leaving at 7pm every day except Wednesdays. The ferry journey takes 16 hours, stopping at two other islands en route, and arrives in Magdiwang mid-morning.

Permits: Not needed.

Equipment: Full camping equipment and food if climbing Mt Guiting Guiting. Good walking shoes, sunblock, insect repellent, leech socks, camera, binoculars.

Facilities: Guides can be hired at the park headquarters; motorized tricycles in Magdiwang for lowland tours; accommodation consists of just a couple of homestays in Magdiwang.

Watching wildlife: Shorebirds can be seen in the mangroves, while raptors can be seen over the forest. Small birds of farmland and forest can be seen in the regenerating lowland forest. It is difficult to see wildlife in the dense forest on the mountain.

Visitor activities: Motorized tours of the lowland areas, birdwatching, hiking.

Above: *Brahminy Kites, frequently seen along Sibuyan's coasts.*

Above right: *Patches of swamp forest adapted to living in marshy condtions, common along Sibuyan's southwest coast.*

Right: *The Rufous Night-heron is rare in the Philippines, but the mangroves of Sibuyan are one place where they can be found.*

Below: *A damselfly found in swamp forest close to Sibuyan's southwest coast.*

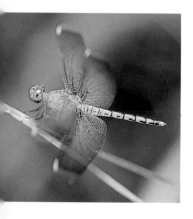

The mangroves in turn give way to seagrass and seaweed beds in the shallow waters, which themselves in deeper water are replaced by a coral reef that encircles much of the island. Along the island's southwest coast mangroves are replaced by specialized beach forest.

For the 47,000 local residents life is basic, consisting of subsistence agriculture and fishing. Almost everyone lives along the coasts, concentrated into three towns, Magdiwang, Cajidiocan and San Fernando. Population growth remains very low, something that has helped preserve the island's natural environment.

Wildlife on the Mountain

The deep waters surrounding Sibuyan have ensured its prolonged isolation, even during the last Ice Age. As a result, it is usually considered a distinct biogeographic zone, as reflected in its mammalian wildlife. Mount Guiting Guiting has been found to harbour no less than five species of mammal unique to the island, four of them small rodents and the fifth a fruit bat. Several other species endemic to the Philippines have been found on Sibuyan, including four fruit bats. One of these, the Philippine Tube-nosed Fruit Bat, was – until recently discovered on Sibuyan – thought to survive only on Negros. Commoner mammals include the Malay Civet and Long-tailed Macaque.

The island's birdlife consists of 131 species, of which 102 are believed to breed here. Birds that can be seen even without climbing to the heights of Guiting Guiting include the Rufous Night-heron, Brahminy Kite,

Wandering Whistling-duck, Blue-naped Parrot and Black-naped Oriole.

Along the shores, Green and Hawksbill Turtles still regularly nest on the beaches, while Olive Ridley, Leatherback and Loggerhead Turtles can be seen occasionally. A few Dugong are present in coastal waters.

Conserving the Island

The protection given to Mount Guiting Guiting came about as a result of a local campaign, fuelled by islanders' fears that excessive logging and harvesting of materials within the forest would destroy the resources on which their already meagre livelihoods depended.

Since the creation in 1996 of the protected area and integration into NIPAP, plans have been put forward to extend the park's boundaries to cover far more of the island's natural treasures. With the park presently covering only 15,700 hectares (38,800 acres), limited to the slopes of Mount Guiting Guiting, most of the lowland forest and all of the mangroves and beach forest fall only within one of the buffer zones, and hence are not fully protected. It is hoped that this will soon be put right.

Exploring Sibuyan

For those keen to climb Mount Guiting Guiting, a trail starts from the park headquarters, close to the north coast and just east of Magdiwang. Although it starts off easily enough, passing through regenerating lowland forest on the coastal plain, it becomes an extremely steep climb, and the round trip requires about three to four days. Rather less long, requiring only 24 hours for the return hike, is the climb to Mayo's Peak, where it is possible to camp overnight and enjoy some simply stunning views.

In the lowlands it is possible to visit a number of waterfalls and explore some of the lowland forest. A few kilometres east of Magdiwang are the Lambingan Falls, the most accessible of all the waterfalls, while a couple of hours' hike to the southwest of the town is Sibuyan's largest waterfall, Cataja Falls, a huge cascade pouring down in several levels through the forest. In the southeast of the island, near San Fernando, is the attractive Lagting Falls, while a little to the west is Cantingas River, a beautiful ribbon of clear water flowing out of the mountains.

Other explorations can take in the mangroves of the north coast and the beach forests of the southwest, as well as some swamp forest, an area of marshy lowland complete with its own specialized forest. Unfortunately, there is no dive operation on the island.

Above: *Beach forest lines a quiet lagoon on Sibuyan Island's southwest coast.*

Left: *A mudskipper, the ubiquitous resident of mangroves, hauls itself up onto a rock at low tide.*

NORTHERN NEGROS FOREST RESERVE

A Forested Volcanic Range

Covering an area of 86,600 hectares (214,000 acres) this mountainous reserve lies approximately 20 kilometres (12 miles) east of Bacolod, capital of Negros Occidental province, in the far north of the island. Proclaimed as far back as 1935, today it protects over half of all Negros's surviving old-growth forest, even though its own forest cover has shrunk considerably over the years. As such, it has become a vitally important reservoir of wildlife, some of it endemic to the Negros-Panay region and now highly endangered.

A Volcanic Landscape

Like much of the Philippines, the whole of Negros is a volcanic land, forming the bulk of the Negros Volcanic Belt, which consists of six volcanoes. Two of these are located on small islands north of Negros while the remaining four are on Negros itself, running the length of the island and forming its north–south mountain spine. Two of these volcanoes lie within the Northern Negros Forest Reserve, 1,534 metre (5,033 feet) Mount Silay and 1,885 metre (6,185 feet) Mount Mandalagan. Both volcanoes

Opposite: *The beautiful Pulang Tubig Falls, one of several that adorn the forests around Patag, in the Northern Negros Forest Reserve.*

Above right: *The Visayan Tarictic Hornbill, endemic to Panay and Negros, is highly endangered but still survives in a few sites on Negros and Panay.*

are inactive, but Mandalagan has fumarole activity in remote forested locations, and both have distinct craters, five in the case of Mandalagan. The landscape also comprises several other distinct peaks, all of which are part of the Silay-Mandalagan volcanic terrain, including Mount Mawa which measures in at just over 1,000 metres (3,300 feet) and Mount Marapara which, at some 1,560 metres (5,120 feet), is higher still.

The Forested Lands

Despite the enormous size of the reserve, only 18,000 hectares (44,500 acres) of old-growth forest remain, most of it in the most mountainous areas above about 800 metres (2,620 feet), the rest having been whittled away by commercial logging and agricultural expansion of the needy rural population. However, the lowest areas of forest, although disturbed, retain some of the largest stands of dipterocarp trees left in Negros, as well as large numbers of the giant Almaciga tree. Above this is a large band of montane forest, characterized by dense stands of tall, straight trees, though smaller than the lowland dipterocarps, and with increasing altitude covered with greater amounts of moss and lichen. Eventually, from an altitude of 1,000 metres (3,300 feet) upwards, this is replaced by mossy forest, a land of dwarf, gnarled trees draped in huge quantities of mosses, ferns and orchids. Around the summits of some of the mountains

Location: Approximately 20 km (12 miles) east of Bacolod, capital of Negros Occidental province, in the far north of Negros Island.

Climate: There is a distinct dry season from December to May. Heavy rain falls from June to November. Typical temperatures in the lowlands are over 30°C (86°F), down to about 20°C (68°F) at Campestuehan or Patag, and at Dinagang Dagat as low as 10–15°C (50–59°F).

When to go: Only attempt to climb during the dry season as the rains make the paths slippery.

Access: Daily flights from Manila to Bacolod, and frequent fast ferries from Iloilo. In Bacolod hire a vehicle. To get to Campestuehan, travel eastwards to Concepcion and then beyond. To get to Patag, travel first to Silay and then head inland.

Permits: Not needed.

Equipment: Good hiking boots, full camping equipment and food if intending to go to Dinagang Dagat, rain-proof clothes, binoculars, camera.

Facilities: Guides can be hired at Patag and Campestuehan, or through the NFEFI or Department of Tourism in Bacolod. Plenty of accommodation in Bacolod. At Patag it is possible to sleep in the old hospital. At Campestuehan it may be possible to stay in someone's home. Plenty of trails radiate out from Patag, fewer from Campestuehan.

Watching wildlife: Dipterocarp and Almaciga forests at low levels. Pines at high altitudes. Forest birds are more visible in the farmland fringes. Visayan Tarictic Hornbills can sometimes be seen around Campestuehan.

Visitor activities: Hiking, bird-watching, visiting fumaroles and waterfalls.

Above: *The Pink-necked Green Pigeon is one of several species of pigeon found in these forests.*

Right: *A spider in its web in lowland forest near the village of Campestuehan*

Right: *The uncurling tips of growing tree fern fronds are just like massive fern fronds.*

Right below: *The Grass Owl hunts over open country at dawn and dusk, roosting in dense grass during the day.*

there are stands of Benguet Pine. None of the mountains has a grassland summit, the dense vegetation making views impossible.

Conservation Work in the Reserve

Much of the work to study and protect the forest is the responsibility of a non-government organization, the Negros Forest and Ecological Foundation, Inc. (NFEFI), based in Bacolod. Its dedicated staff, helped by an international team of scientists, has launched an ambitious programme not only to protect the remaining forest but also actually to expand it through restoration of some damaged areas.

The work has entailed developing an inventory of the reserve's fauna and flora, as well as improving protection measures through a system of forest guards combined with alternative livelihood training programmes for local communities. This last facet of their work is designed to help those living on the mountains' slopes make an environmentally sustainable livelihood without continually cutting away more and more forest.

Moreover, with help from Britain's Fauna and Flora International, NFEFI has recently established a captive breeding programme for some of the area's most endangered wildlife, including the Visayan Spotted Deer, the Visayan Warty Pig and the Visayan Taritic Hornbill, all animals that are highly endangered but which are believed to survive in the Northern Negros Forest Reserve. The breeding programme is based in a compound adjacent to the NFEFI office in Bacolod and is open to visitors.

Exploring the Forest

There are two areas accessible to visitors, the slopes of Mounts Marapara and Mandalagan directly east of Bacolod, and an area known as Patag on the slopes of Mounts Silay and Mandalagan, northeast of the city. To reach the former, one travels to the village of Campestuehan in the barangay of Concepcion. Here the motorable track ends next to an abandoned school, now used by NFEFI. From here it is possible to hike along trails that lead into healthy dipterocarp and Almaciga forest, and then through dense montane forest and onto the slopes of Mount Mandalagan. Visayan Taritic Hornbills can sometimes be seen in the forest close to Campestuehan. Deep into the mountainous interior, in a narrow valley known as Dinagang Dagat, is an active fumarole perpetually pouring out sulphurous smoke and steam. Close by is an attractive lake, located at an

Above: *Densely forested Mt Mawa, on the edge of the Northern Negros Forest Reserve, towers over the village of Campestuehan.*

altitude of 1,432 metres (4,698 feet), which usually dries up during the dry season to form grassland. This area is a convenient camp site in which to spend the night before returning to Campestuehan, or to use as a base for exploring the surrounding mossy forest.

Patag is reached via Silay, a coastal town north of Bacolod. A motorable road comes to an end close to an abandoned hospital, now used as a registration and starting point for hikers heading up onto Mount Silay. Guides can be hired here. In this area hiking trails are well developed, with a sketch map available showing approximate hiking times. This region is a waterfall-lover's heaven, for there are at least three within an hour's walk of the hospital. The longer trails head up through dense forest to stands of Almaciga trees, and at the highest levels to a ridge covered in pine forest. One trail links up with Dinagang Dagat, thus making it possible to hike between Campestuehan and Patag.

Left: *The Visayan Warty Pig, as its name implies, is restricted to the Visayan islands. Though endangered, they frequently raid village fields on the edge of the the Northern Negros Forest Reserve.*

Left below: *The Visayan Spotted Deer is another Visayan endemic. Extremely shy, it is restricted to the remoter parts of the forest.*

MOUNT KANLAON NATURAL PARK

The Visayas' Highest Mountain

Situated in the central-northern region of Negros, Mount Kanlaon is one of six volcanoes that form the Negros Volcanic Belt, part of which is submarine but whose bulk is visible as Negros's mountainous spine. Kanlaon is presently the only active volcano in this chain, its last eruption having been in 1996.

Consisting of dense rainforest as well as the volcano, and covering an area of 24,600 hectares (60,700 acres), this is one of the Philippines' ten priority protected areas, a group of the country's most important parks in the Integrated Protected Areas System (IPAS), established in the mid-1990s. Unlike most of the other priority protected areas, however, Mount Kanlaon has been a reserve for quite some time, having been proclaimed a national park as far back as 1934.

A Wild and Primeval Landscape

This highly active volcano is defined as a stratovolcano, which means it has the potential for serious, violent eruptions. In fact, although it has erupted frequently, in recent history all eruptions have thankfully been quite small ones.

Opposite: *The gaping chasm that is the active crater of Mt Kanlaon, highest mountain and most active volcano in the Visayas.*

Above right: *Signs encouraging respect for nature at Mambucal hot spring resort.*

As with most Philippine volcanoes, the terrain is extremely steep, culminating in the active crater at the summit, variously reported as between 2,438 and 2,465 metres (7,999–8,088 feet) high, making it the highest mountain in the Visayan region. The active crater is a fearsome sight, a gaping hole estimated to be 500 metres (1,640 feet) across, with sheer walls that plunge directly into an apparently bottomless funnel from which curls a small but constant plume of smoke and steam. There is no flat area around the rim of the crater; instead the outer slopes leading up to it end abruptly in a knife-edge rim that actually overhangs the chasm. There is no vegetation here, only grey volcanic rock, the loose gravelly surface making it essential to take care while walking.

North of this crater is an old, inactive crater known as the Margaha Valley. Now green and pleasant, its southern end is carpeted with grass which turns into a lake approximately a metre (3 feet) deep during the rainy season. Further north again is a secondary peak, Mount Makawiwili, and beyond this the mountain slowly descends in a series of steps marked by ancient volcanic craters, now mostly beautiful lakes, towards the hot spring resort of Mambucal.

Conserving the Forest and Its Wildlife

Since 1934 half of the park's 24,600 hectares (60,700 acres) has been converted to farmland by encroaching settlers. However, the remaining 11,500 hectares

Location: Central-northern Negros, approximately 30 km (19 miles) southeast of Bacolod.

Climate: A dry season from January to May, with heavy rains from June to December. Temperatures at the base of the mountain range from 30°C (86°F) to 37°C (96°F), falling quickly with altitude to about 15°C (59°F) at 1,500 metres (4,900 feet) and lower still at the summit.

When to go: Climb only in the dry season. The mountain is closed to hikers during the rains.

Access: Daily flights from Manila to Bacolod. From here take a shuttle bus to La Carlota and then a jeepney to Guintubdan. Return to Bacolod from Mambucal by jeepney.

Permits: Obtain from the Natural Park office in Bacolod. Permits will be checked at the park office in Guintubdan.

Equipment: Good walking boots, full camping equipment, food and fuel, waterproof and warm clothing, leech socks, insect repellent, camera, binoculars.

Facilities: Guides and porters can be hired through the Department of Tourism office in Bacolod. Camping grounds at Guintubdan and five sites along the route. The trails are very simple and unmaintained. Hotels in Mambucal, plus excellent hot springs.

Watching wildlife: Dipterocarp, montane and mossy forests, with a range of flowering plants, rattans and vines. Animal wildlife difficult to spot, but some forest birds may be visible. Fruit bats can be seen at Mambucal.

Visitor activities: Soaking in the hot springs, hiking, photography.

(28,400 acres) are still densely forested, and include the three main bands of forest, namely lowland evergreen forest, montane forest and mossy forest. Although rather fragmented by agricultural encroachment and further damaged on the mountain's northern slopes by the recent construction of a geothermal plant, parts of the lowland forest still consist of the characteristic triple canopy. The tallest trees, as much as 37 metres (120 feet) high and forming the upper canopy, are the dipterocarps, consisting of *Shorea* and *Parashorea* species, in the Philippines commonly known by such names as Lauan, White Lauan and Tanguile, all important timber trees now quite rare owing to the massive and chronic logging that has occurred throughout the country. Below these is a layer of shorter trees, up to 20 metres (65 feet) high, which make up the majority of the forest's tree species. The third and lowest canopy consists of immature trees of both these groups.

At approximately 1,000 metres (3,300 feet) this forest gives way to montane forest, consisting of a two-layer forest of trees up to 20 metres (65 feet) high, as well as large numbers of Pandanus plants, both as free-standing shrubs and climbers, climbing bamboo, rattans and other palms, and a wide variety of vines. Flowering plants can sometimes be seen, especially the now quite rare *Medinilla magnifica*, known locally as Kapa-Kapa, an epiphyte with clusters of pink flowers that usually hang down from the trees above. As one climbs higher and rainfall increases, so does the amount of moss on the trees. Above approximately 1,800 metres (5,900 feet) one is in the realm of the mossy forest, consisting of only a single storey of dwarf trees, draped in mosses. There is also a wealth of other vegetation, including pitcher plants, staghorn and ribbon ferns, and orchids, including the rare Waling-Waling more commonly associated with Mindanao.

About 50 species of bird have been identified on the mountain, including the Flame-templed Tree Babbler, rhe White-winged Cuckoo-shrike and the Visayan Tarictic Hornbill, believed to be restricted on Negros to just a few sites. Only 11 species of mammal are so far known in this area, but these include the Visayan Spotted Deer and the Visayan Warty Pig, both highly endangered, as well as the Malay Civet, the Leopard Cat and five species of fruit bat.

Hiking on the Volcano

There are several routes up this mountain. One of the best, which involves camping out for two nights, starts

from the village of Guintubdan on the western slopes. There are several attractive waterfalls in this area, and the village is renowned as the fighting cock breeding capital of Negros – it is hard to imagine so many cockerels in one place! From here the path strikes out into dense montane forest and climbs steeply all the way to the ridge that surrounds the Margaha Valley, leading to the active crater.

After visiting the summit, backtrack along the ridge and then follow a path past the Makawiwili peak and through dense mossy forest towards Samoc Lagoon, remnant of an ancient crater and a beautiful lake with a pleasant camping area. This is an exhausting section of the path as one is constantly climbing over or under low and fallen trees, but as the dense mossy forest is left behind so the trail becomes rather easier, and as it dips down to approximately 800 metres (2,600 feet), so one enters dipterocarp forest.

Reaching the new geothermal installation signals that the hike is nearing its end; a couple of hours later you pass the Wasay entrance to the park and soon are descending into the very pleasant little hot spring resort of Mambucal – the ideal place for a long soak after the exertions of the trail.

Above: *The Margaha Valley, the remains of an old crater, close to the summit of Mt Kanlaon.*

Left: *A wild hydrangea in flower in Kanlaon's dense montane forest.*

Left: *Wild ginger in flower in dense montane forest.*

Opposite: *Magasawang Falls, a gem hidden in the forest just a few minutes' walk from Guintubdan.*

DANJUGAN ISLAND MARINE RESERVE AND WILDLIFE SANCTUARY

Conservation on a Tiny Island

Lying just off the southwest coast of Negros, this tiny island is something of a gem in that not only is it surrounded by a fringing reef that is adorned with a wide variety of corals, but also because it is still completely forested and is thus home to quite an array of wildlife. Although in the 1980s it began to suffer increasing environmental damage, since the mid-1990s the island has become the focus of an energetic conservation programme that has recently seen it officially classified as a protected area.

A Diverse Environment

Danjugan (pronounced 'Danhoogan') is barely more than a speck of land 1.5 kilometres (1 mile) long and 500 metres (550 yards) wide at its widest point. Yet within that small space is a dense forest growing over a series of steep razor-sharp limestone hills, no less than five lagoons ringed with mangroves, several caves and a number of beaches. The forest and mangroves are home to an estimated 68 species of bird (not bad for such a tiny piece of land), ranging from minute

Opposite: *The coastline of Danjugan Island, with surf breaking on its fringing reef, a forested jewel of an island off the southwest coast of Negros.*

Above right: *A Lumnitzera mangrove tree in flower.*

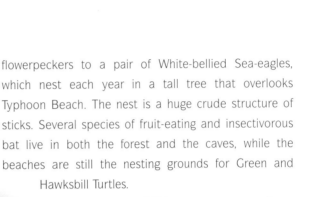

Manta Rock
Manta Island   Lagoon 1
⋀ Camp
Danjugan Island
Marine Reserve
and Wildlife
Sanctuary
Andrea's Reef
Tangiguigi Reef
Lagoon 2
Lagoon 3
Lagoon 4   Convention Reef
Lagoon 5
N
Twin Peaks
Manila
Negros
Malaysia
To Bulata →
Hilary's Rock
Twin Ridge
Doug's Ridge

flowerpeckers to a pair of White-bellied Sea-eagles, which nest each year in a tall tree that overlooks Typhoon Beach. The nest is a huge crude structure of sticks. Several species of fruit-eating and insectivorous bat live in both the forest and the caves, while the beaches are still the nesting grounds for Green and Hawksbill Turtles.

Offshore, surveys have found that the coral reefs are home to an estimated 240 species of coral (out of a national total of 450 species), belonging to 72 genera, and about 230 species of fish.

The island is not in a pristine state, however. There has been some logging, and the reefs have been damaged by dynamite and cyanide fishing, inflicted mainly in the 1980s when closure of a local quarry caused both unemployment and a flood of dynamite and cyanide into the community. Two severe typhoons also caused further damage, largely as a result of silt washed down into the sea from deforested hills on the nearby mainland. Moreover, the waters have been heavily overfished. This is the result partly of incursions by outside commercial fishing operations, and partly of the efforts of local fishermen, most of them from the nearby mainland village of Bulata, simply in their struggle to make a living.

Location: Three km (2 miles) off the southwest coast of Negros, opposite the village of Bulata, and 150 km (90 miles) south of the provincial capital, Bacolod.

Climate: The dry season lasts from November to May, the rainy season from June to October or November. Daytime temperatures are at their coolest in January–February, at about 30°C (86°F), and reach 34–36°C (93–97°F) in May. Sea breezes help to keep nights reasonably cool. Humidity is always high, at 80–90%.

When to go: The dry season is definitely the best time. Sunny weather does occur during the rainy season, but frequent violent storms can cut the island off for days and make life very difficult.

Access: From Manila there are daily flights to Bacolod. From here, frequent buses run to Sipalay, passing Bulata en route. It may be necessary to change bus in Kabankalan. From Cebu, fly to Bacolod or take a high-speed ferry to Dumaguete in southeastern Negros. From here take a bus to Kabankalan and then change to another heading for Sipalay. To reach Danjugan Island, hire a boat in Bulata.

Permits: From the Philippine Reef and Rainforest Conservation Foundation Inc, in Bacolod.

Equipment: Walking shoes, swimsuit, snorkelling and/or diving gear (nothing available at Bulata at the time of writing), sunblock and insect repellent.

Facilities: Accommodation in Bulata and Sipalay. Boats for hire at Bulata. A few footpaths on Danjugan.

Watching wildlife: White-bellied Sea-eagles, fruit bats, various forest birds, limestone forest, mangroves, marine turtles and a range of reef fish and corals.

Conservation Work on and around Danjugan

In 1995, the newly formed Philippine Reef and Rainforest Conservation Foundation Inc (PRRCFI), a non-government organization based in Bacolod, the provincial capital in the north of Negros, bought the island with help from the British organization the World Land Trust. Since then the PRRCFI has been engaged in an imaginative and so far successful conservation programme designed both to restore Danjugan's environment and to improve the livelihoods of the local fishermen.

The first stage of the programme was to develop an inventory of the island's wildlife. For this a series of Filipino and overseas scientists studied the terrestrial environment while the British group Coral Cay Conservation brought in an endless supply of willing volunteers to map and survey the surrounding reefs. These studies went hand-in-hand with community work to gain the support of Bulata's fishermen, increase general awareness of the need to protect the environment, and begin the process of developing alternative, or additional, livelihood skills among the local people.

Already the project is starting to bear fruit, with the fishermen themselves setting up several sanctuaries around Danjugan's coast in which fishing is strictly banned, along with a large buffer zone in which only fishing with hand-lines is allowed. It has been claimed that fish yields have already started to rise, although frequent monitoring by Coral Cay Conservation has yet to confirm

this. Their beachside camp, over which towers the tree in which the White-bellied Sea-eagles nest, has recently been converted into a small field studies centre, complete with accommodation for visiting students and conservationists. Community work, especially alternative livelihood development, is ongoing, and the project is now starting preparations for reforestation of the denuded mainland hills above Bulata and the nearby town of Sipalay.

Whilst it is true that on a national scale the Danjugan project is very small, it will hopefully serve as a model to be replicated throughout the entire Philippines, thus allowing many similar environments to be restored while at the same time improving the economy of the local people themselves.

Visiting the Area

Until recently, the only accommodation was in Sipalay 10 kilometres (six miles) south along the coast from Bulata, making it difficult to stay in the Bulata/Danjugan area itself. Recently, however, a small resort has opened at Bulata, and another will do so soon on an island close to Danjugan. Both resorts are claimed to be environmentally friendly developments in tune with

the aims of PRRCFI. While Bulata is a typically poor but lively and friendly fishing village, retreating to the uninhabited islands leaves one with only the noises of the forest and sea. On approaching Danjugan by boat, one becomes slowly aware – as the forest comes closer and towers ever higher above – of the mixture of bird and insect song pouring out from among the trees, a symphony of noise rarely heard in the coconut groves and scrublands around the mainland villages. At night this music fades away to be replaced by the croaking of frogs and the silent light show of thousands of fireflies, pinpricks of moving incandescence that mingle beautifully with the stars.

Left: *Overseas conservation workers prepare for inventory work on one of Danjugan's coral reefs.*

Below: *A common, primitive coral reef animal, a large and colourful* Polycarpa tunicate.

Below: *An expanse of* Lithophyton *soft corals – typical of a reef recovering from past damage.*

SOUTHERN NEGROS FOREST RESERVE

Forest, Lakes and Volcanoes

Situated in the far south of Negros, this volcanic landscape towers over the city of Dumaguete, capital of Negros Oriental province. Consisting of two main mountain peaks, collectively known as Cuernos de Negros – the 'Horns of Negros' – and a number of lakes, this is the southern-most of six volcanoes that make up the Negros Volcanic Belt. The Southern Negros Forest Reserve is one of only three significant blocks of old-growth forest remaining in Negros and hence is of major conservation importance.

A Volcanic Landscape

The Cuernos de Negros volcano climbs up directly from the southeastern coast of Negros, with the pleasant university city of Dumaguete sitting at its feet. The highest points of this landscape are

Opposite above: *Lake Balinsasayao, surrounded by lowland forest and dominated by the peaks of Cuernos de Negros.*

Opposite below left: *The fruits of a Pinanga palm, in dense montane forest on the slopes of Mt Talinis.*

Opposite below right: *Although orchids are common, most are epiphytic, growing from tree trunks and branches. Ground orchids, such as this one on Mt Talinis, are less common and not easily seen in flower.*

Above right: *A damselfy close to the shore of Lake Balinsasayao.*

the volcano's twin peaks, Mount Talinis at 1,870 metres (6,135 feet) and Mount Chesco at 1,650 metres (5,414 feet). Although inactive, there is still considerable geothermal energy evident around the volcano, with fumaroles on its lower southeastern slopes near the town of Valencia (a nearby installation taps this source).

Several lakes mark the sites of ancient volcanic craters, amongst which two, Lakes Hulawig and Yagumyum, lie between the two peaks and a third, Lake Nailig, is found on the summit of Mount Chesco itself. The largest lakes, however, are Danao and Balinsasayao, collectively known as the Twin Lakes, which lie close together at an altitude of only about 800 metres (2,600 feet) in the northeastern part of the reserve, 10 km (six miles) north of Mount Talinis.

Forest and Wildlife

Dense old-growth forest surrounds the mountain peaks and lakes, covering an area of 4,000 hectares (10,000 acres). The lower areas, mainly around the Twin Lakes, still have extensive stands of dipterocarp lowland rainforest, as well as patches of Almaciga, the largest tree in the Philippines (which can grow up to 60 metres/197 feet in height). Most of the forest, however, especially on the slopes of Mount Talinis, consists of montane and mossy forest, with vegetation around the peak of Talinis itself consisting largely of junipers.

Location: In the far south of Negros, 15 km (9 miles) west of Dumaguete, Negros Oriental provincial capital.

Climate: The dry season lasts from January or February to May. The rainy season lasts throughout much of the rest of the year. Temperatures at the base of the mountain range from 30°C (86°F) to 37°C (96°F), falling quickly with altitude to approximately 15°C (59°F) at the summit.

When to go: Visit during the drier times. Talinis is still climbable when a little wet, but the four-wheel-drive track to Twin Lakes quickly becomes impassable in rain.

Access: Daily flights from Manila to Cebu, followed by high-speed ferry to Dumaguete. Also regular, but not daily, flights from Manila to Dumaguete. To reach Twin Lakes, hire a guide and four-wheel-drive vehicle. To climb Talinis from Camp Lookout, hire a guide, take a jeepney to Valencia and then tricycle to the trailhead.

Permits: Not needed.

Equipment: Good hiking shoes, full camping equipment and food if intending to stay overnight, waterproof clothing, camera, binoculars.

Facilities: Simple, unmaintained paths. Plenty of accommodation in Dumaguete. Camping possible beside Lake Yagumyum.

Watching wildlife: Different forest types at Twin Lakes and Mt Talinis. Animal wildlife is extremely difficult to see, although some birds may be visible in the forest. Some of the mammals can be seen in captivity at the Center for Tropical Conservation Studies in Dumaguete.

Visitor activities: Birdwatching, boating on Lake Balinsasayao, hiking on Mt Talinis.

Above: *In the dense forest on Mt Talinis, it is common for hikers to lose sight of each other.*

Above right: *The Yellow-breasted Fruit Dove, though widely hunted, still finds a home on Mt Talinis.*

A series of studies has found that even this rather limited forest area contains a wide range of animal life, much of it rare and almost all dependent on the forest remaining healthy. Thus, 50 of the 102 species of bird, 12 of the 24 mammals, and 37 of the 68 amphibians and reptiles so far identified are Philippine endemics. Among the birds seven of the endemic species are actually restricted just to Negros, and at least 10 are threatened to varying degrees, including the Visayan Writhed-billed Hornbill and most especially the Negros Bleeding-heart Pigeon. Birds more commonly seen in the reserve include a variety of endemic flowerpeckers, the Metallic Wood-pigeon and the Philippine Hanging-parrot or Colasisi.

The endemic mammals include the Visayan Spotted Deer, the Visayan Warty Pig, three rodents and eight species of fruit bat, including the world's largest bat, the Golden-crowned Flying Fox. Other mammals are

Leopard Cat, Palm Civet and Malay Civet, although they are uncommon in the reserve.

Despite the forest's great conservation importance, it is slowly shrinking owing to the pressure of the surrounding population. At present conservation efforts are fragmented, although a number of non-government organizations as well as staff at Silliman University and the Center for Tropical Conservation Studies (Centrop), both based in Dumaguete, are involved in community work aimed at helping local communities develop alternative, more environmentally sustainable livelihoods.

Exploring the Lakes and Mountains

Two of the most interesting areas to explore are the Twin Lakes and the slopes of Mount Talinis. The first is reached via a long and very rough four-wheel-drive track that ends beside a small lake at the forest-farmland boundary. From here it is a short hike through a mixture of farmland and forest to the shore of Lake Balinsasayao, where it is usually possible to hire a local farmer to row one across the lake in a tiny outrigger canoe. The lake is a glorious sight, a large expanse of rippled blue water surrounded by dense green dipterocarp forest, with the peaks of Cuernos de Negros looming above. Once on the far shore it is another short hike across a saddle to the smaller Lake Danao.

Several trails climb Mount Talinis, the most accessible starting from Camp Lookout, close to Valencia. It is possible to climb to the summit and return to Dumaguete in a single day, but the terrain makes for an exhausting hike. The first hour of the hike is across farmland, but once inside the forest it quickly becomes very dense and largely undisturbed, initially montane forest with trees 15–20 metres (50–65 feet) tall, but later becoming mossy forest, with dwarf trees only three to four metres (13 feet) tall. From a ridge that was once cleared, the view across Dumaguete and the sea beyond used to be stunning, but today the forest has fully regenerated and once more enclosed the path. A little further along the path splits, one trail heading down into a valley to the shore of Lake Yagumyum, the other continuing onwards for a couple more hours to the summit. After all the effort of climbing to this great height, one might hope for a spectacular view, but even here the vegetation crowds in around the path. The lakeshore makes for a pleasant campsite, and anyone intending to visit both lake and summit would be advised to stay there overnight.

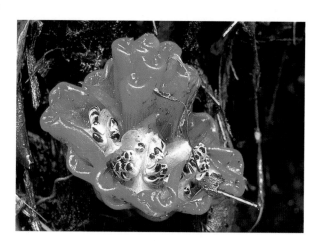

Above: *A local farmer quickly fashions a new paddle from a tree branch before taking his boat out across Lake Balinsasayao.*

Left: *Forest floor vegetation, consisting mainly of Alocasia, in Talinis' montane forest.*

Left: *The fruiting body of a wild ginger, growing directly from the ground, in the forest on Mt Talinis.*

APO ISLAND PROTECTED LANDSCAPE AND SEASCAPE

One of the Earliest Marine Reserves

Not to be confused with Apo Reef off the west coast of Mindoro, this small 75 hectare (185 acre) volcanic island lies close to the southeastern tip of Negros, seven kilometres (4 ¼ miles) from the nearest mainland town, Malatapay. Site of one of the country's first and to date most successful marine reserves, established in 1985, more recently – in 1995 – the entire island was given protected area status. A result of the long-standing marine protection is a series of reefs teeming with life, from the tiniest corals to the largest deep-water fish. Inevitably, therefore, Apo is becoming an increasingly popular dive site, with dive boats frequently visiting the island from the nearby towns of Dumaguete and Dauin.

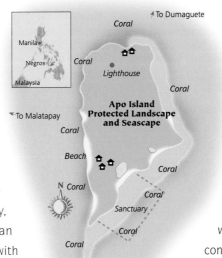

Opposite above: *Elaborate vase sponges are common around Apo Island, especially along its southwest coast.*

Opposite below left: Dendronephthya *soft tree corals, barely more than a few inches tall, are commonly found along Apo Island's western side.*

Opposite below right: *An* Atriolum *tunicate, or sea squirt, a common resident of Philippine reefs.*

Above right: *Barrel sponges, often as much as one metre (three feet) high, can be found at many sites around the island's coastline.*

A Reef and Island Environment

Roughly oval, with its axis running north–south, this is a rocky island with two hills, the northernmost the highest at about 200 metres (660 feet). Between the hills the land is flat, forming something of an isthmus between the east and west coasts. Much of this flat land is occupied by the island's village, home to over 400 people. Both hills are covered with secondary scrub, along with a few fields growing a variety of crops. On the eastern edge of the island are two lagoons lined with mangroves, separated from the sea by a steep, pebbly beach. The western shore, where the main part of the village is concentrated and where all boats come ashore, consists of a mixed sandy and rocky beach.

The island is completely surrounded by a fringing reef, consisting in most places of a fairly narrow reef flat at a depth of approximately five to seven metres (16–23 feet), followed by a reef crest that gives way to a wall or steep slope dropping down to 30 metres (100 feet) or more. The reef on the island's eastern side looks quite different from that on the west, the latter consisting mostly of a slope rich in soft corals, the former of huge, mostly volcanic boulders, covered with hard corals and comparatively fewer soft corals. Surrounded by deep water, Apo's reefs are notorious for their ferociously strong currents, usually running from north to south, and often switching direction in localized eddies.

Location: Off the southeastern coast of Negros, 7 km (4.3 miles) east of Malatapay, and 25 km (15.5 miles) south of Dumaguete, capital of Negros Oriental province.

Climate: The rainy season lasts from June to December, the dry from January to May. The wind blows from the northeast from June to October or November, and from the southwest for the rest of the year.

When to go: April–May provides the sunniest weather and calmest seas, but this is also the hottest time. November–March is cooler, but strong northeasterly winds may make the sea rough. June to October is mostly calmer, with rain and the risk of typhoons.

Access: Daily flights from Manila to Cebu, followed by high-speed ferry to Dumaguete. Daily flights from Manila to Bacolod, followed by express bus to Dumaguete. Regular, but not daily, flights from Manila direct to Dumaguete. Dive operators in Dumaguete and Dauin will provide transport to the island, either their own boat or one hired in Malatapay. If making your own way, go to Malatapay and hire a boat.

Permits: Not needed.

Equipment: Swimsuit, sunblock, camera, waterproof bag, footware. Diving equipment can be hired.

Facilities: Dive operators in Dumaguete and Dauin. Two small resorts on Apo Island with their own diving facilities. Plenty of boats to hire at Malatapay. Plenty of good hotels in Dumaguete, resorts in Dauin.

Watching wildlife: A vast array of fish and coral life; especially butterflyfish, Moorish Idols, groupers and wrasse. Also shoals of barracuda and jacks.

Visitor activities: Diving, swimming, photography and walking.

Above: *The island's western shore, a mixture of coral sand and rock, is the main landing site both for local fishermen and dive operators.*

Below: *Black-tip Groupers are a common sight around coral reefs.*

A Model for Reef Protection

In the early 1980s, scientists from Silliman University in nearby Dumaguete began to work on a programme to protect Apo Island's reefs. Through community work with the island's residents they were able to gain widespread support for the idea. In 1985 the local government proclaimed all the waters around the island, to a distance of 500 metres (1,640 feet) offshore, a marine reserve in which only traditional hand-line fishing methods were allowed. On the island's southeastern side 280 hectares (700 acres) were designated a marine sanctuary in which all fishing was banned. At the time the reefs received protection there was some dynamite and cyanide damage, so part of the conservation programme consisted of seeding the damaged areas with new corals.

Since then the reserve and sanctuary have been managed and policed by the islanders themselves, and over the years their fish catches have more than doubled. In 1995 the Department of Environment and Natural Resources declared the entire island a protected area, as well as the surrounding sea, naming it a protected landscape and seascape.

There seems to be little doubt that the combination of marine reserve and sanctuary has worked extremely well, the total protection of both corals and fish enabling them to breed in the sanctuary and then spread to other areas of the reef. In recent years, the increasing numbers of visiting divers seem to have been the main source of damage to Apo's reefs, inflicted by anchors and clumsy divers. The first of these problems may have been overcome by the recent introduction of mooring buoys at each dive site, thus removing the need for anchors.

Diving Around and Exploring Apo Island

Although a very small island, the fact that it is completely surrounded by a reef ensures that there are several good sites to head for. Almost all visits to Apo include a dive in the sanctuary, as well as other parts of the island, although exact locations depend very much on currents and sea conditions. Every dive site consists of a wide variety of healthy hard and soft corals and sponges, and one encounters miniature canyons of huge rocky blocks covered in brain and staghorn corals.

Fish life is abundant all around the island, but especially so inside the sanctuary. Everywhere one finds a multi-coloured array of such reef fish as butterflyfish, Moorish Idols, damselfish, tubefish, wrasse, groupers, fusiliers and triggerfish. Large squid and sea snakes are also present. The strong currents mean that the reef attracts the many of the deep-water varieties of fish, such as shoals of barracuda, tuna and jacks, which are commonly seen, especially in the sanctuary, while Whitetip and Blacktip Reef Sharks are encountered from time to time.

If your dive boat lands on the island between dives, take the chance to explore. It is only a few minutes on foot from the western beach through the village to the mangroves on the eastern shore, an enjoyable walk that will provide a view of the islanders' life. Alternatively, a concrete path leads to the top of the northern hill, through some dense secondary scrub.

Above: *A shoal of barracuda.*

Below left: *A group of divers prepares to dive in Apo Island's sanctuary.*
Below: *A diver swims over a stand of* Lithophyton *soft corals.*

OLANGO WILDLIFE SANCTUARY

A Major Wetland Habitat

A 920 hectare (3,950 acre) protected area at the southern end of Olango Island, off Cebu's east coast, this is the Philippines' most important site for migratory wetland birds. First given protected area status in 1992, it became what is known as a Ramsar site in 1994, an international status that registered Olango Island as a conservation site of global importance.

Mudflats and Mangroves

Olango is a very low-lying island, 7.5 kilometres (4 ¾ miles) long and three kilometres (2 miles) wide at its widest point, situated six kilometres (3 ¾ miles) southeast of Mactan Island, on Cebu's east coast. About 16,000 people live here, mainly in the northern half, while the southern part consists of a large and very shallow bay containing a vast area of mangroves and mudflats. It is here that the wildlife sanctuary is situated.

Opposite above: *Mangroves standing on the edge of a vast expanse of sand and mud.*

Opposite below: *Pandanus trees adorned with colourful fruits thrive in the poor soil lying just inland of Olango's mangroves.*

Above right: *Egrets are among the migratory birds commonly seen at Olango.*

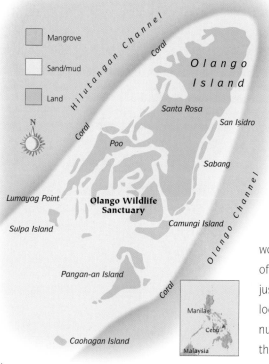

Olango is an important part of the East Asian Flyway, the route along which thousands of birds travel between summer breeding grounds in northeast Asia, and overwintering areas to the south and in Australasia. An estimated 40,000–60,000 waders and other shore birds either make this their winter home or rest here while en route between sites further north or south. Not surprisingly, peak times for birds at Olango depend on the migration schedules, with September to November for the southward migration, and between February and April for the northward journey.

The area is rich in molluscs, worms and the fry for a huge array of sea life, making it important not just for the visiting birds but for the local human population too. As a nursery, the sanctuary provides the young fish that maintain much of the local fishing industry, and as a site rich in shellfish it directly provides a major source of protein and income for the islanders. Every day at low tide, local people can be seen out on the mudflats collecting shellfish, something that does not seem to disturb the flocks of birds unduly.

There have been several plans to convert this entire environment into fish and shrimp ponds, something that would be a disaster for wildlife and local people alike. However, now that it has Ramsar protected status it is to be hoped that any such destructive developments will be impossible.

Location: 6 km (3.7 miles) southeast of Mactan Island, off the east coast of Cebu. It is easily visible from many of the resorts on Mactan Island.

Climate: The dry season lasts from January or February to May. The rainy season is from June to December or January. Daytime temperatures range from 30°C (86°F) in January to 37°C (98°F) in May. Humidity is always high, at at least 80%.

When to go: For birdwatching go during the peak times for bird migration: September to November and February to April.

Access: Daily flights from Manila to Cebu, Mactan International Airport. Frequent high-speed ferries from Tagbilaran (Bohol) and Dumaguete (Negros) to Cebu. Travel to Santa Rosa on Olango by ferry from Maribago on the east coast of Mactan. Take a tricycle from Santa Rosa wharf to the nature centre.

Permits: Obtainable from the Protected Environments and Natural Resources Office of the Department of Environment and Natural Resources, in Cebu City.

Equipment: Shoes that are good for walking in mangroves and salt water; drinking water; insect repellent; hat; binoculars; camera (with telephoto lens); camping equipment and food if hoping to stay on Olango overnight.

Facilities: Accommodation on Mactan Island and in Cebu City. No accommodation on Olango Island. Nature centre in the sanctuary.

Watching wildlife: A wide range of birds, including egrets, Redshanks, plovers, tattlers and Asian Dowitcher.

Visitor Activities: Walking, birdwatching.

Species to be Found

The mangrove areas have been found to consist of 23 species of tree and associated plants (such as climbers specialized to mangrove areas), the most common belonging to the *Rhizophora* genus. Most trees are less than two metres (six feet) high, unusually small for mangroves in the midst of the tropics. It has not yet been established whether this is due to natural local conditions or excessive past cutting. The area is also rich in marine algae and seagrasses, of which 16 species have been found so far.

Almost 100 hundred species of bird have been counted in the sanctuary, 42 of them terrestrial and the remainder associated with water. Easily seen waterbirds include a wide range of well-known and common species, such as several species of plover, tern, Knot, Redshank, Whimbrel, stint and egret. Several rare, endangered species are also commonly found here, including Asian Dowitcher, Chinese Egret and Eastern Curlew. Other species that can sometimes be seen include Mangrove Heron, Cinnamon Bittern and Garganey. Amongst the commonest of the terrestrial birds, usually seen in the mangroves and surrounding scrubby woodlands, are Barn and Pacific Swallows, but others include Brown Shrike, Olive-backed Sunbird and Collared Kingfisher.

Exploring the Sanctuary

Olango is easily reached by ferry from Mactan Island. There is a nature and ranger centre on the western side of the sanctuary, so any tour should start here. At low tide the birds disperse across the mud and sandflats, so it is difficult to get close views. It is possible to approach reasonably close by walking slowly across the mud, but visitors are discouraged from doing this for fear of disturbing the birds. Closer views are possible when a rising tide drives the birds towards the mangroves.

Above: *Mangroves, ringed by pneumatophores that enable the trees to obtain air even when immersed, lie spread across large areas of Olango Island's mudflats, making a perfect environment in which migratory wading birds can rest and feed.*

Below: *An assortment of waders make use of Olango's shallow waters and extensive mudflats as feeding grounds during the winter months.*

PESCADOR ISLAND MARINE RESERVE

Pristine Reefs in the Tanon Strait

The tiny island of Pescador, the pinnacle of a submarine mountain rearing up from the depths of the sea, is surrounded by a spectacular reef that teems with a vast array of marine life. Although occupying a fairly small area, along with a number of other nearby reefs this is one of the best diving sites in the country. Situated on the southwest coast of Cebu, approximately 90 kilometres (55 miles) from Cebu City and reached via the small town of Moalboal, it is also one of the most accessible.

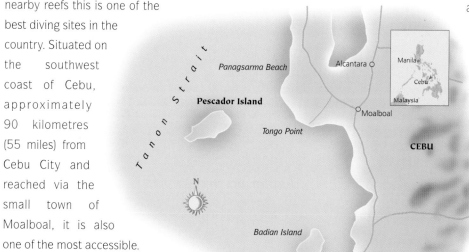

Rugged Underwater Terrain

Pescador Island lies in the southern part of the Tanon Strait, a narrow but extremely deep stretch of water separating Cebu from Negros to the west. Although only approximately 28 kilometres (17 miles) wide, the straits form a major trench that plunges to a depth as great as 550 metres (1,800 feet). Although Pescador lies just 2 kilometres (1 ¼ miles) off Cebu's west coast, the water between it and the mainland reaches a depth of 300 metres (1,000 feet)!

The island itself is barely 100 metres (110 yards) long and rises just six metres (20 feet) above the sea. Its shore consists entirely of a sheer coralline limestone cliff, undercut at sea level, and its surface is flat, covered with

Above right: The ubiquitous lionfish lurks among the dense stands of hard corals at relatively shallow depths.

rough, scrubby vegetation. It is completely surrounded by a narrow reef about 100 metres (110 yards) wide, which slopes gently from a depth of about three metres (10 feet) down to nine metres (30 feet) before reaching the reef crest. This gives way to a vertical wall that plunges to a depth of 40 metres (130 feet) on the east and west sides and 50 metres (160 feet) at the island's northern end. The walls contain a huge number of ledges, overhangs and crevasses, although the most spectacular natural formation is the Cathedral, a huge funnel that is open at the top and on its side at a depth of 15 metres (49 feet), and which bottoms out at a depth of 34 metres (112 feet).

A Wealth of Marine Life

This reef is home to a vast array of corals, which crowd against each other right across the whole reef flat, and which on the crest form a dense forest of plates, branches and fronds that ends abruptly at the edge of the wall. Here you will find virtually every variety of hard and soft coral known in Philippine waters, from the large table and staghorn Acropora corals, to the huge bulbous brain corals, the aptly named mushroom corals, the tiny globules of bubble coral, and the upright, stinging plates of the fire corals. On the walls are huge Gorgonian sea-fans, testament to the strong currents that sweep around

Location: In the southern part of the Tanon Strait, separating Cebu from Negros; 2 km (1 ¼ miles) off the southwest coast of Cebu. The nearest mainland town is Moalboal.

Climate: The dry season lasts from February or March to May. The rainy season lasts from June to January or February, although most rain falls from July to October. Daytime temperatures vary from about 30°C (86°F) in January to 37°C (98°F) in May. Humidity is always high, at least 80%.

When to go: The area can be dived at any time, but for assured sunny weather go in April or May, although this is also the hottest part of the year.

Access: Daily flights from Manila to Cebu. High-speed ferries from Tagbilaran (Bohol) and Dumaguete (Negros) to Cebu City. Take a bus from Cebu City's South Bus Terminal to Moalboal (3 hours), and tricycle from Moalboal to Panagsama Beach.

Permits: Not needed.

Equipment: Sunblock, hat, camera, swimsuit. All diving and snorkelling equipment can be hired.

Facilities: Accommodation, restaurants, boat hire and dive shops at Panagsama Beach. Diving courses available.

Watching wildlife: A huge variety of marine life around Pescador Island's reef, from sharks to gobies and many corals. Boat trips to look for dolphins and whales in the Tanon Strait.

Visitor activities: Diving, snorkelling, swimming, dolphin and whale watching. Nearby mountain biking and hiking.

Above: *A group of Long-snouted Spinner Dolphins makes its way through calm waters in the Tanon Strait, separating Cebu from Negros.*

Above right: *In Moalboal, accommodation comes right down to the edge of Panagsama Beach.*

Pescador, as well as a range of soft tree corals, black corals, sponges and nudibranchs.

The pristine condition of Pescador's reef ensures that it teems with reef fish. The list of species is virtually endless, but among the most obvious are Fire Gobies, Bluestreak Gobies, angelfish, butterflyfish, Moorish Idols, soldierfish, wrasse, groupers, sweetlips, batfish, pufferfish and lionfish. Being completely surrounded by very deep water, shoals of pelagic fish are common, especially jacks, barracuda, snappers and fusiliers. Tuna are also often seen in these waters, and Whitetip, Grey and Hammerhead Sharks come by from time to time. Several species of dolphin and small whale live in the

Tanon Strait, and although they are not usually seen while diving around Pescador Island they are often visible from a boat.

Diving on the Reef

The nearest diving operations are based at Panagsama Beach, about four kilometres (2.5 miles) away on the Cebu coast, near the little town of Moalboal. Here lodges, restaurants and dive shops are strung out along the shore for several hundred metres, catering mostly to visiting divers. The beach here was destroyed by a major typhoon in 1984, so there is little beach life for the non-diver to enjoy.

Right: *Pescador Island's reef crest consists of an astonishingly dense and varied mass of hard corals, inhabited by huge numbers of small reef fish.*

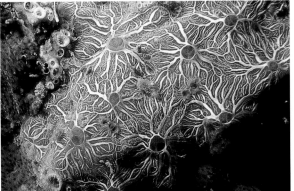

Above: *Pescador Island is little more than a small, raised coralline limestone platform.*

Far left: Tubastraea *cup corals keep their tentacles withdrawn if the current is slack.*

Above left: *A beautiful pink sponge,* Clathria mima, *clings to rocks in relatively shallow waters.*

Almost everyone diving here will pay at least one visit to the Cathedral, but apart from that dives consist of drifting along the walls, rising up onto the prolific reef crest and flat towards the end of each dive.

When not diving, boat trips can be arranged to look for dolphins and whales – and sightings of large schools of Spinner Dolphins are virtually to be guaranteed in this area – while on the mainland, for the more energtic, mountain biking or even hiking expeditions can be organized.

Left: *Detail of Favites coral, a very common hard coral that forms large domes covered with this pattern.*

EASTERN VISAYAS AND MINDANAO

Although geographically rather distinct from one another, the eastern Visayas and Mindanao form a single major biogeographic zone, usually called the Greater Mindanao Faunal Region. This is because all these islands were linked by land bridges during the last Ice Age 18,000 years ago, a time when sea levels were 120 metres (400 feet) lower than today. As a result, they have a similar fauna, which is also related to some extent to that of Borneo and Sulawesi. Thus, two of this area's characteristic mammals, the Philippine Tarsier and Philippine Flying Lemur, both endemic to the Greater Mindanao Faunal Region, are closely related to similar species found in Borneo. Apart from Bohol, much of this region has still to be fully explored, and there are a number of large forest areas as yet unprotected which may well prove to be of great importance to conservation. Mount Kitanglad and Agusan Marsh are classic examples of this, both regions that were almost completely unknown until the late 1980s or even early 1990s, but which are now vital parts of the country's new Integrated Protected Areas System (IPAS).

Much of the landscape is rugged, with the Kitanglad range and Mount Apo, the country's two highest mountains, cutting across large parts of Mindanao. This is one reason why study has been limited, but another has been the region's long-running insurrections that came to an end only in the early 1990s.

Visitor facilities can be quite limited in or around some of the protected areas but there is the excitement of knowing that this is the frontier of conservation, spiced with the anticipation that more fascinating areas may become accessible in the future.

SOHOTON NATIONAL PARK

Gorges and Limestone Caves

Sometimes also called Sohoton Natural Bridge National Park owing to a natural rock formation that forms a natural bridge across a gorge, this national park lies in the southern part of Samar. Established in 1935, its 840 hectares (2,075 acres) take in some attractive limestone gorges and caves, as well as lowland limestone rainforest which, despite the park's small size, is home to an interesting array of wildlife.

A Limestone Landscape

Several rivers carve through this area, creating gorges and caves out of the permeable limestone. The park's main feature, situated in a gorge and close to the banks of the Cadacan River, is Panhulugan I Cave, a complex labyrinth of tunnels and chambers filled with stunning stalactite and stalagmite formations. Many of the most prominent have been given names that supposedly match their appearance, such as the Banaue Rice Terraces, Great Wall of China, Sitting Madonna and the King's

Opposite: *Pristine stalactite and stalagmite formations are typical of Sohoton's Panhulugan I Cave.*

Above right: *The Long-tailed Macaque is a common animal in Sohoton.*

Previous pages:
Page 110: *Mangroves, interspersed with coralline rocks, lie in a quiet cove on Siargao Island.*
Page 111: *A ground orchid growing on the edge of forest on Mt Malindang.*

Throne. Although Panhulugan I Cave is the most visited and largest cave, there are others in the park, including Panhulugan II, Sohoton, Bugasan and Kapitagan. A number of archaeological finds have been made in the caves, including human teeth (some of them decorated), and numerous shell bracelets, beads and iron fragments. Chinese ceramic jars, possibly used as burial urns and bearing Ming Dynasty (14th–17th century) decorations have also been found, suggesting more recent occupation. During the Second World War, the caves were used as hide-outs by anti-Japanese resistance fighters.

Three kilometres (2 miles) upriver from Panhulugan I Cave the 120-metre (394 feet) natural rock bridge – complete with forest vegetation on its upper surface – spans the gorge above the river, presumably a rare survivor of thousands, if not millions, of years of erosion from rain and at one time the force of a running river. Four kilometres (2 ½ miles) beyond this is Cabungaan Waterfall, an 80-metre (260 feet) cascade set in dense forest and located on the furthest edge of the national park.

The Park's Wildlife

Although covering a rather small area, much of the park is densely covered with lowland dipterocarp forest adapted to the limestone conditions. This has given some of the trees enormous buttress roots to help hold them in the thin soil, but in turn has prevented them from growing into the giants normally associated with lowland evergreen rainforest. The fauna is typical of the Greater Mindanao region, with Tarsiers and Flying Lemurs present, as well as

Location: In southern Samar, northeast of Basey at 11°22'N 125°10'E.

Climate: The region has no clearly defined dry season, although most rain falls in November–December. The driest month is April. Daytime temperatures range from 30°C (86°F) in January to 34°C (93°F) in May. Humidity is always high, usually over 80%.

When to go: The caves may be closed during the height of the rainy season. The river level should be high enough to explore upriver from Panhulugan I Cave at the end of the rainy season, perhaps in February or March.

Access: Frequent flights from Manila to Tacloban. Regular fast ferries from Cebu City to Ormoc and then express connecting bus to Tacloban. From Tacloban take a jeepney or boat to Basey and then hire a boat for the journey to and from the park.

Permits: Obtainable in Basey at the Community Environment and Natural Resources Office (CENRO).

Equipment: Good shoes, binoculars, camera, torch (flashlight), drinking water and food for one day.

Facilities: Accommodation in Tacloban only. Boats and guides for hire at Basey. Park rangers will guide you, with a lamp, through the caves. Picnic area outside Panhulugan I Cave. Footpath between the natural bridge and Cabungaan Waterfall.

Watching wildlife: Monitor lizards and sometimes macaques can be seen around the picnic area. Specialized insects and spiders inside Panhulugan I Cave.

Visitor activities: Boat riding, cave exploring, walking.

monitor lizards, Long-tailed Macaques, wild boar and Palm Civets. The Rufous Hornbill and Blue-naped Parrot are believed to live in this forest, and there has even been one reported sighting of a Philippine Eagle close to Panhulugan I Cave, back in 1985.

Boating and Caving

The park is most easily reached from Tacloban, the largest city on Leyte. From there you travel by boat or jeepney to the township of Basey, situated on the southwest coast of Samar, and then by boat up the Cadacan River for about 90 minutes before reaching the park. A permit should be obtained at Basey's Community Environment and Natural Resources Office (CENRO). The boat journey from Basey is an adventure in itself, starting out in the Cadacan River's estuary before pushing upstream past mangroves frequented by egrets. The river is lined by mangroves and later nipa palms for much of the journey, apart from occasional villages and views of low-lying farmland on both sides. Fishermen can frequently be seen on the river, working with lines or small nets from tiny outrigger canoes.

Approaching the park, the river starts to twist among hills that are increasingly forested and which soon turn into limestone cliffs, leading through a small gorge. Eventually, the boat arrives in a natural amphitheatre with a landing stage hidden in one corner – the entrance to Panhulugan I Cave. At a small picnic area outside the cave but sheltered by dense trees a ranger will check your permit and then lead you on a tour of the cave. Lighting is provided by the guide's powerful kerosene lamp, so it is important to stay quite close to him – there is no other lighting and no paths cut through the cave. Stalactites and stalagmites, some tiny, some huge ancient columns, adorn every passage and chamber, many marked with cascading, flowing patterns that suggest the movement of water 'frozen' in time forever. Coloured brilliant white, golden and brown, many sparkle in the lamplight, adding more than just a touch of magic to the scene. There is wildlife even in here; keep a look out for specialized spiders and giant millipedes that lead their entire lives in this darkness.

Beyond the cave, if the river level is high enough it is possible to continue by boat upriver to the natural bridge. With low water levels, alas, this journey is not possible, and with no footpath there is no way to walk to the bridge from Panhulugan I Cave. From the natural bridge onwards the river is always too shallow for boats, but at this point a footpath starts, leading right up to the natural bridge and then pushing on through dense forest for several kilometres to Cabungaan Waterfall.

Above: *The Philippine Tarsier, at barely 7cm (3 inches) long, excluding its tail, is one of the world's smallest primates. It is spread throughout the Greater Mindanao region.*

Right: *Cave spiders are amongst several invertebrate species perfectly adapted to life in the darkness of Panhulugan 1 Cave.*

Left: *Access to Panhulugan I Cave is by boat, which ties up in a wide part of the river, ringed by limestone cliffs.*

Below: *Extensive stalactite and stalagmite formations in Panhulugan I cave, the most accessible of Sohoton's caves.*

BALICASAG ISLAND MARINE RESERVE

Submarine Cliffs Teeming with Life

Location: Approximately 8 km (5 miles) southwest of Duljo Point on Panglao Island, Bohol, at 9°31'N 123°41'E.

Climate: The dry season lasts from January to June, with rains for the rest of the year. The peak of the rainy season is from August to November, and the driest months are April and May. Daytime temperatures range from 30°C (86°F) to 35°C (95°F), the hottest time being May.

When to go: For diving, the high season is November to May. Strong northeast winds can sometimes make diving around Balicasag difficult in December–February. The calmest months are April–May.

Access: Daily flights from Manila to Cebu, followed by high-speed ferry to Tagbilaran, capital of Bohol. High-speed ferries also run daily to Tagbilaran from Cagayan de Oro and Camiguin Island, Mindanao, and from Dumaguete on Negros. From Tagbilaran take a tricycle or taxi to Alona Beach, and then go with a dive boat.

Permits: Not needed.

Equipment: Swimsuit, sunblock, sunglasses, hat, camera. All snorkelling and diving equipment can be hired on Alona Beach or at the Balicasag Island Dive Resort.

Facilities: One resort on Balicasag Island; plenty of accommodation at Alona Beach, Panglao Island. Numerous dive operations on Alona Beach, one at Balicasag Island Dive Resort.

Watching wildlife: A vast array of marine life to be seen underwater, whether diving or snorkelling.

Visitor activities: Sun-bathing, swimming, snorkelling, diving.

This is a tiny island lying southwest of Bohol, about eight kilometres (five miles) from Panglao Island, site of Alona Beach, Bohol's most popular beach resort. The island itself is flat and low-lying, covered with coconut palms and rough scrub, but it is ringed by a dazzlingly white beach and beyond that by some of the Philippines' most stunning submarine scenery. A narrow coral reef, surrounding much of the island, ends abruptly in massive walls that drop into deep water, teeming with life. These waters became a marine reserve in 1986, and include a fish sanctuary on the southwestern side in which no fishing of any kind is allowed.

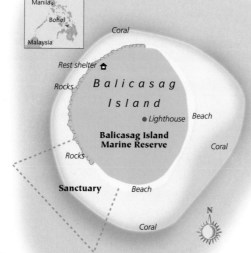

A Tiny Desert Island

A rather featureless piece of land, Balicasag is a perfectly flat, almost round island, barely 600 metres (650 yards) in diameter and covering an area of approximately 30 hectares (75 acres). Despite its isolation from

Opposite above: *The shore of Balicasag Island, surrounded by a dazzling white beach.*

Opposite below left: *Detail of a beautiful, translucent* Dendronephthya *soft tree coral.*

Opposite below right: *A deadly scorpionfish lies close against the rock and coral, extremely well camouflaged against its background.*

Above right: *A Fromia starfish, common inhabitants of Balicasag's coral reefs.*

Panglao Island, it is inhabited by about 60 families, who inevitably make their living from fishing. Although these people have come to live here at some point in the past 50 years, the island has been occupied since the 1870s, when a watchtower was built to guard Bohol against Moslem attacks from Mindanao. To this day the island remains a naval reserve, administered by the Philippine Coastguard. A small lighthouse was built on the island in 1907, a beacon that still lights the sea lanes for shipping travelling to and from Cebu.

For the visitor, apart from a small resort run by the Philippine Tourist Authority, the only interesting feature of the island itself is the astonishingly white beach made of coralline sand, billions of tiny white fragments of the reef that encircles the island. The beach is particularly fine close to the resort, making an excellent base from which to go snorkelling.

Conservation of the Island's Waters

The fringing reef, walls and drop-offs that surround Balicasag have long been recognized for their vast range of marine life. As early as the 1970s the area was recommended as a possible marine park, but little happened until 1984 when staff from the Marine Laboratory at Silliman University, based in Dumaguete on Negros, began their Marine Conservation and Development Programme. This consisted of community work aimed at encouraging the local populations of three islands –

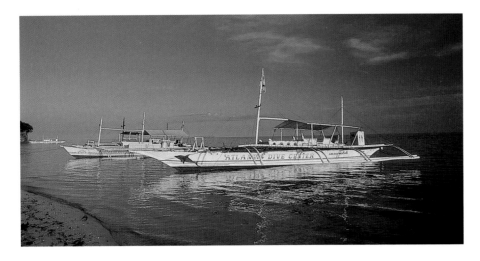

Balicasag, Pamilacan (to the south of Bohol) and Apo (south of Negros) – to launch and maintain their own reserves. The work was successful, resulting in the fishermen of Balicasag establishing their own marine reserve late in 1985, gaining official status in 1986.

The reserve consists of all the waters around the island to a distance of 500 metres (550 yards) offshore, covering an area of 150 hectares (360 acres), along with a fish sanctuary of eight hectares (20 acres) off the southwest shore. Within the former only traditional hand-line and trap methods of fishing are allowed, while in the latter all fishing is banned, providing a sanctuary in which both fish and corals can breed safely, allowing them to spread to adjacent areas of the reef.

The reserve and sanctuary are still policed by the islanders themselves. Visiting dive boats have to pay a fee for the privilege of diving in the reserve and are allowed only to tie up to one of the few buoys placed for the purpose – no anchors are allowed.

Diving Among the Marine Life

The reef begins in the shallows immediately off the island's beach, and extends to a distance of 50–100 metres (55–110 yards) from the shore and to a depth of 7–11 metres (23–36 feet) before the reef crest is reached, followed by a wall or steeply sloping drop-off. Along the southern side of the island the reef terminates at the edge of an absolutely vertical wall, which drops from a depth of about eight metres (26 feet) straight down to 35 metres (115 feet), while on the north side the drop-off is a slope.

The reef is populated with all the usual hard corals, including staghorns, table corals, brain corals, fire corals, fungus and mushroom corals, while on the walls and slopes are multicoloured Gorgonian sea-fans, soft tree corals, whip corals, nudibranchs and sponges. The northern slope is also well known for its forests of black corals, characterized by masses of long coralline 'fronds' or 'tentacles'. In this area the sandy bottom is home to hundreds of garden eels, which partially extend from their homes in the sand, forming a forest of 'sticks' waving in the currents, instantaneously retracting en masse into the sand the moment they are disturbed.

Fish life is truly massive and includes everything from the tiniest gobies to sharks. It is always possible to see a vast range of reef fish, including striped lionfish, multicoloured wrasse, Moorish Idols, small and larger groupers, sweetlips and pufferfish. Frogfish and even scorpionfish, both almost invisible as they crouch low

and almost perfectly colour-matched against their background, are quite common. Banded sea snakes are also a regular sight; although they have never been known to attack divers, they are best left alone.

The deep waters off the reef ensure that large numbers of pelagic fish frequent Balicasag. Shoals of Trevally, jack and barracuda are commonly seen, often forming huge 'walls' of fish, as well as incredible spiral columns, vertical tubes created by hundreds of fish swimming in circles. It is possible for divers to enter these tubes to experience a huge column of fish endlessly circling all around.

Opposite, top: *Dive boats moored at Alona Beach, ready for the next day's dive trips to Balicasag.*

Opposite, bottom: *A novice diver receives training in Balicasag's shallows.*

Above: *Most people intending to visit Balicasag Island stay on Alona Beach, a 45-minute boat ride away.*

Below left: *A diver has an encounter with a Banded Seasnake off Balicasag Island.*

Below right: *Stinging hydroids are to be avoided as even a gentle brush can give bare skin a very nasty sting.*

Above: *A* Xenia *soft coral, typified by this much-branched form crowned with long, waving polyps and coloured creamy-white is ubiquitous, found on just about every Philippine reef.*

Right: *A shoal of Big-eye Trevally, seen against a high sun, sweep across above the diver, a common sight in the deep waters around Balicasag Island.*

Below: *Living close to the reef, and using its many nooks and crannies for shelter, is a myriad of small, multi-coloured fish.*

RAJAH SIKATUNA NATIONAL PARK

A Limestone Forest
Close to the Chocolate Hills

Situated on the island of Bohol, this national park is named after the Boholano chieftain who in 1565 made a blood compact with Miguel Lopez de Legaspi, founder of the first permanent Spanish settlements in the Philippines. Declared in 1987, the park covers 9,000 hectares (22,300 acres) of hilly limestone forest in the south of the island, and is very close to the far more famous Chocolate Hills, a strange landscape of naturally rounded hills that is one of Bohol's best-known visitor attractions.

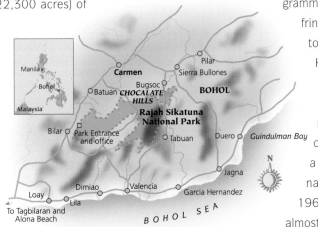

A Unique Primary Forest

Much of Bohol has been deforested for quite some time, as far back as the 19th century. Today, the forest within Rajah Sikatuna National Park

Opposite above: The view from Bod Daku, highest point in the accessible area of the park, across to farmland outside the park's boundaries.

Opposite below left: A stinkhorn fungus growing out of the forest floor. The unpleasant smell it emits attracts flies that help to spread its spores.

Opposite below right: A young rattan, a slow-growing climbing palm used extensively for furniture production, starts its climb towards the forest canopy.

Above right: A butterfly takes a rest. Well-protected forests like Rajah Sikatuna are an important refuge for many of the Philippines' unique species of forest butterflies.

represents the last of the island's primary rainforest, occupying just four per cent of its land area. A considerable amount of work seems to have gone into ensuring that its protection works, with a number of well-established plantations and reforestation programmes operating around its fringes. Anyone travelling towards the Chocolate Hills from Tagbilaran will pass through one of these plantations, the road south of the town of Bilar twisting through a dense rainforest, originally planted in the 1960s and now seemingly almost mature.

The landscape consists of a large number of mostly small limestone hills ranging in altitude from 200 metres (660 feet) to 800 metres (2,625 feet), almost all covered in dipterocarp forest. Most of the trees are small by the usual standards of primary evergreen lowland rainforest, owing to the limestone substrate that ensures a very thin soil and little water.

Tarsiers and Flying Lemurs thrive here, the latter often seen leaping among the trees at dusk, the former sometimes visible on tree-trunks at night. In addition, there are also Malay and Common Palm Civets, wild boar, monitor lizards, Long-tailed Macaques and several species of fruit bat. The macaques are quite tame and frequently to be found around the picnic area.

It is for its bird population that Rajah Sikatuna is most renowned. Among the total species count, an astonishing 48 Philippine endemic species have been

Location: Central-southern Bohol, with the entrance on the western edge, at Bilar, 35 km (22 miles) northeast of Tagbilaran, Bohol's capital.

Climate: The rainy season lasts from July to January, with most rain falling in October or November. The period from February to June is dry. Daytime temperatures range from 30°C (86°F) in January to 34°C (93°F) in May.

When to go: It is better to visit during the dry season as paths can be very slippery in the rain. However, the forest is much lusher during wet periods.

Access: Daily flights from Manila to Cebu. From here take a regular fast ferry to Tagbilaran. From Tagbilaran either hire a vehicle or take a bus bound for Carmen, get off at Bilar and hire a motor tricycle to take you into the park.

Permits: Obtainable on arrival in the park.

Equipment: All food, drinking water, torch (flashlight), candles, stove and sheet if intending to stay in the park overnight; good walking shoes, binoculars, camera, hat, insect repellent, swimsuit.

Facilities: Plenty of accommodation in Tagbilaran and Alona Beach, Panglao Island. A couple of basic bungalows and a dormitory in the park. Well-laid and signposted footpaths. A cooling swimming pool. A leaflet is available describing the park and containing a simple map.

Watching wildlife: Around the picnic area macaques are common, and Flying Lemurs can be seen at dusk. A wide range of bird life may be visible.

Visitor activities: Swimming, bird and macaque watching, hiking.

Right: *The Mindanao Bleeding-heart Pigeon is an endangered species endemic to Greater Mindanao.*

Far right: *Unique to the Greater Mindanao area, the Philippine Flying Lemur can often be seen at dusk gliding among the trees around Rajah Sikatuna's picnic area.*

found here, including two that are entirely restricted to the eastern Visayas, plus all four subspecies endemic to Bohol. Twelve species are listed in the Philippines Red Data Book and are thus in some danger of extinction. The endemic species commonly found here include Philippine Serpent-eagle, White-eared Brown-dove, Philippine Hawk-owl, Philippine Frogmouth, Philippine Bulbul and Coleto.

Exploring the Park

Rajah Sikatuna National Park is probably one of the most easily visited of the country's protected areas. The western end of the park lies close to Bilar and the main road linking Tagbilaran to the Chocolate Hills. A new motorable track leads from the main road right into the park, where a forest clearing contains a picnic area, nature office, aviaries and a couple of very basic bungalows for hire. From here, 30 kilometres (19 miles) of well-laid hiking trails – including handrails and steps cut into the steepest hillsides – lead out into the western part of the park, allowing visitors a good taste of Sikatuna's forest while leaving much of it quite inaccessible. The paths are signposted, making this one of the few places in the Philippines where a guide is not needed. The terrain is quite rugged, one of the paths climbing to a watchtower built on Bod Daku, the highest point in this part of the park, at 560 metres (1,837 feet) above sea level. And it is also possible from here to enjoy a spectacular view across forested hills and the rice farmlands around nearby Bilar. For those needing a cool soak after a tiring hike, an attractive swimming pool has been created right on the park's edge, where forested hillside meets flat ricefields. The water comes from three natural springs on the nearby forested hillside, and is channeled directly to the pool.

The picnic area is one of the best sites for wildlife watching. Not only are many birds more visible here than in the depths of the forest, but also the site is regularly visited by macaques, while at dusk the open tree canopy is a good place in which to see Flying Lemurs take to the air.

Below: *Where the protected forests of Rajah Sikatuna meet low-lying rice fields, an attractive swimming pool has been built, fed by three nearby springs.*

MOUNT MALINDANG NATIONAL PARK

A Major Watershed Forest

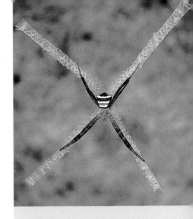

Declared a national park in 1971 and covering 53,260 hectares (131,600 acres), this mountain is a major watershed in western Mindanao, providing clean water and flood control for a number of nearby coastal cities, including Dipolog, Oroquieta and Ozamis. One of the very few protected areas in this part of Mindanao, it is also of great importance to local wildlife, and for this reason has been incorporated into the new European Union-funded National Integrated Protected Areas Programme (NIPAP).

A Little-Known Region

More a range than a single mountain, the park is rectangular in shape, oriented north–south, with the range's eastern, more accessible, slopes rising abruptly from a flat coastal plain approximately nine kilometres (5 ½ miles) wide. There are four main mountain peaks, called North Peak, South Peak, Mount Ampiro and Mount Malindang itself. Malindang is the highest, reaching 2,404 metres (7,888 feet), with North Peak coming next at 2,237 metres (7,340 feet). Eight rivers drain the mountain range and there is a lake, called Lake Dinagat, at 2,100 metres (6,890 feet) near North Peak.

The mountain was extensively logged before being designated a national park, so although some areas of old-growth forest remain, much that is accessible is now secondary growth. Furthermore, two villages have been

Above right: A spider in its web awaits its prey.

established in the northern part of the park, resulting in the loss of some previously forested areas to farmland. Most of these people are migrants who have moved into Mindanao from other parts of the Philippines, but there is also one long-established tribal group, the Subanon, who consider the whole of the Malindang range to be their tribal homeland.

While logging once formed a major part of the economy, today it is farming, relying on annual crops such as rice, vegetables and maize (corn), and on permanent plantations of coconut, fruit, coffee, rubber and Manila hemp. Illegal logging still continues on a small scale, as do hunting and the collection of non-timber forest products, including orchids, rattans and medicinal plants.

Fauna and Flora

Over 30,000 hectares (74,000 acres) of the park remain densely forested, rendering the park of great importance to wildlife conservation. While the lower slopes of the mountain, outside the national park, were long ago converted to farmland and coconut plantations, in more recent years even areas up to and over 1,000 metres (3,300 feet) above sea level have been affected by logging and slash-and-burn farming, producing large areas of grassland and forest fragments. At 800–1,500 metres (2,600–4,900 feet) there is some secondary dipterocarp forest, but in many places extensive forest does not start until the montane forest area is reached, above

Map labels:
Manila
Mindanao
Malaysia
MINDANAO
Mount Malindang National Park
To Dipolog
Jimenez
Sinacaban
Tudela
Iligan Bay
Glarin
To Cagayan de Oro
Ozamis
Mt Malindang 2425m (7956ft)
Embargo
Sitangit
Tangub
Bonifacio
Balatacan
Disum
Tubod
Baroy
Panquil Bay
Aurora
Kapatogan

Location: In Misamis Occidental province, western Mindanao. The nearest city is Ozamis, on the coast of Iligan Bay.

Climate: There is no pronounced wet or dry season, but the wettest period is July to January. Daytime temperatures at the foot of the mountain are 30–35°C (86–95°F), and about 10°C (18°F) cooler in the montane forest area.

When to go: The mountain can be visited at any time of year, although rain can be expected at any time, with the driest weather likely from February to May.

Access: Regular flights from Manila and Cebu to Dipolog and Cagayan de Oro, followed by express bus to Ozamis. At the time of writing flights from Manila to Ozamis have been discontinued. In Ozamis, hire a vehicle for the journey to Hoyahoy, and a guide for exploring the forest.

Permits: At the time of writing not needed, but visit the national park office in Ozamis for help in finding a guide.

Equipment: Hiking boots, hat, binoculars and camera. If intending to stay on the mountain overnight complete camping gear and all food will be needed.

Facilities: Accommodation in Ozamis, transport for hire to reach the mountain, and trails into the forest above Hoyahoy.

Watching wildlife: Some forest birds should be visible, but it is often difficult to see much in the dense vegetation. Serpent-eagles are often seen circling overhead.

Visitor activities: Birdwatching, photography, hiking.

Above: *A Fomus* fungus, a species commonly seen growing on tree trunks in dense forest.

Above right: *The fruits of the* pinanga *palm, a variety frequently found in montane forest.*

1,500 metres (4,900 feet). Above 2,000 metres (6,560 feet) mossy forest extends all the way to the summits.

Within this forest there is still quite an array of wildlife, including the endangered and endemic Philippine Eagle. Other endangered birds that have been seen on Mount Malindang are Rufous Hornbill, Mindanao Bleeding-heart Pigeon and Philippine Cockatoo. Mammals include Philippine Tarsier, Philippine Flying Lemur, Philippine Deer and the ubiquitous Long-tailed Macaque. Studies of the plants have so far found 16

Right: *A young Philippine Deer, a species that is widespread right across the country, though nowhere is it common.*

Far right: *A civet, another species that is spread across much of the country, can be found on Mt Malindang.*

key, or rare, species, including a begonia and three species of orchid found only in the forest.

Visiting Mount Malindang

The park is most easily reached from the coastal city of Ozamis, located near the southern end of the mountain range. From here, a road leads via Tangub up into the southeastern sector of the park, to the tiny village of Hoyahoy. From the village a trail leads across steep grasslands towards the edge of a huge gorge at the foot of which is the Labu River, and then upwards along the edge of the gorge and into dense montane forest. From here the forest can be explored for quite some distance, but the path eventually peters out. There is no trail to any of the summits, and one must return down the same route.

From a point just below the edge of the forest, a viewing area is under construction, giving superb views across Ozamis and the blue waters of Panguil Bay far below. The park management is planning to build a ranger station here. This will enable them to issue permits and to charge fees to visitors wishing to explore the forest for themselves.

Above: *Montane rainforests on the middle slopes of Mt Malindang, an important wildlife refuge and watershed for western Mindanao.*

Left: *The Coleto is a type of forest starling endemic to the Philippines.*

Left: *A mantis stalks almost invisibly among grass on the forest fringe.*

MOUNT KITANGLAD RANGE NATURAL PARK

Home of the Philippine Eagle

This mountainous area in the north-central region of Mindanao, covering much of the province of Bukidnon, is one of the Philippines' most important forested parks. Declared a natural park in 1990, it is known to be a stronghold of the endangered Philippine Eagle and to contain one of the most complete forest ecosystems in the country. Covering an area of some 30,650 hectares (75,720 acres) the park contains more than a dozen high peaks. The highest is Mount Dulang-Dulang, at 2,938 metres (9,640 feet) the second highest mountain in the Philippines. Mount Kitanglad itself comes close behind at 2,899 metres (9,512 feet). The park is designated as one of the country's ten priority protected areas in the Integrated Protected Areas System.

A Rugged Mountain Range

The Kitanglad range forms the highest and one of the wildest parts of a volcanic highland landscape, known as

Opposite above: *Mt Kitanglad's montane forest canopy, home to the Philippine Eagle.*

Opposite below left: *A wild balsam, or* Impatiens, *growing in Kitanglad's forest.*

Opposite below right: *An* Aeschynanthus *flower growing in montane forest undergrowth.*

Above right: *Pineapples are grown in vast plantations beneath the Mt Kitanglad range.*

the Lanao–Bukidnon Highland, which stretches across much of central Mindanao. The natural park, along with its 14,480 hectare (35,780 acre) buffer zone, is more or less an oval shape with its long axis oriented east–west, lying just to the west of Malaybálay, the Bukidnon provincial capital. The park's highest peaks are all concentrated in the eastern half of the park, and include not only Mounts Dulang-Dulang and Kitanglad, but also Kaatuan and Maagnaw.

For anyone arriving in the park from the east, the first peak encountered is that of Mount Apolang. Though relatively small, it remains prominent for its very dense and healthy rainforest, unusual in this area, close to the buffer zone and where there has been plenty of disturbance. The reason for its survival in good condition is its sacred stature among the local communities.

Fauna, Flora and their Conservation

It has been estimated that more than 25,000 hectares (62,000 acres) of the park are covered by old-growth forest, with another 11,500 hectares (28,400 acres) consisting of open-canopy forest or brushland, most of this within the buffer zone. The latter consists almost entirely of evergreen lowland forest damaged by slash-and-burn farming practised by encroaching settlers. Within the park proper, evergreen lowland forest, containing many large dipterocarp trees, continues up to an altitude of about 1,400 metres (4,600 feet), before it is replaced by montane forest. This in turn gives way to a

Map labels:
Manila
Mindanao
Malaysia
MINDANAO
To Cagayan de Oro
Capihan
Kalilangan
Dahilayan
Intavas
Dalwangan
Mount Kitanglad Range Natural Park
N
Mt Nanluyaw
Mt Kitanglad 2899m (9512ft)
Mt Maagnaw
Mt Dulang-Dulang 2938m (9640ft)
Mt Kaatuan
Mt Apolang
Lalawan
Malaybalay
Baylanan
Sangaya
Victory
Sungco
Alanib
To Kidapawan

Location: In Bukidnon province, central-northern Mindanao, directly west of Malaybalay, Bukidnon provincial capital, and 50–60 km (31–37 miles) in a straight line southeast of Cagayan de Oro.

Climate: Rain falls throughout much of the year, although there is a short dry season February–April. March is the driest month, June the wettest. Daytime temperatures at the lower altitudes range from 25°C (77°F) in January to 30°C (86°F) in June. At Lalawan temperatures may drop to about 12°C (54°F) at night, and lower still at higher altitudes.

When to go: Visit in the drier periods. During the rains the paths become extremely slippery.

Access: Regular flights from Manila and Cebu to Cagayan de Oro. From here, express buses take two hours to Malaybalay. From Malaybalay jeepneys ply to the villages on the fringe of the park. To reach Lalawan, head to Dalwangan, just north of Malaybalay, and then hike 8 km (5 miles).

Permits: No need, but always take a guide (visit the KIN office in Malaybalay for help).

Equipment: Hiking boots, rainproof clothing and rucksack, all food, leech socks, camping equipment and stove, camera and binoculars.

Facilities: Numerous trails. Guides and accommodation available in Malaybalay. PEFI has a simple lodge at Lalawan, which visitors may be allowed to use. Visit their office in Malaybalay to enquire.

Watching wildlife: Philippine Eagles can sometimes be seen near Lalawan. Other eagles may also be seen, along with forest birds.

Visitor activities: Birdwatching, camping, hiking.

mossy forest at 1,800–2,000 metres (5,900–6,600 feet), which continues most of the way to the summit.

Within these forests, and also along the agricultural fringes, surveys conducted in 1992 and 1993 found 134 species of bird, including the Philippine Eagle and 16 of Mindanao's 17 endemic birds. Moreover, 58 species of mammal were identified, mostly rodents, including three new to science of which, so far as is known, at least one is unique to the Kitanglad range. A number of these avian and mammalian species, such as Philippine Deer, wild pig, hornbills and racquet-tailed parrots, have been badly over-harvested for food and the pet trade in other parts of the Philippines, yet seem to maintain good populations here.

The surveys also showed quite clearly that much of the wildlife is restricted to specific altitudes within the range, thus stressing the need to protect the forest at all levels in order to ensure protection of this vast biodiversity. Unfortunately, the lowland evergreen forest is under increasing pressure from farmers and continued illegal logging. It is shrinking annually, and in a few places has disappeared altogether, farmland now reaching up as far as the fringes of the montane forest. As a worrying indication of this, the 1992-3 surveys also found that 20 species of bird identified in the 1960s and 1970s, and known to be restricted to the lowland evergreen forest, could no longer be found.

To counter this, a number of non-government organizations (NGOs), including the Philippine Eagle Foundation, Inc. (PEFI) and Kitanglad Integrated NGOs (KIN), have become very active in helping the communities around the park to develop environmentally sustainable

livelihoods that do away with the need to cut down the forest. Their projects usually involve growing permanent crops, such as coffee and Manila hemp, as well as setting up cooperatives to help market the final products. It is still early days, but it is to be hoped that such programmes will help to ensure the park's protection.

Hiking the Range

Attractions within the park include a number of trails that allow exploration of and birdwatching within the forests, especially at lower altitudes, plus tracks leading to the summits of Mounts Kitanglad and Dulang-Dulang.

The park is most easily approached from Malaybalay and the main road that runs north towards Cagayan de Oro. From the village of Intavas, close to the northern edge of the park, a trail leads to the summit of Mount

Kitanglad. It is a steep route, but because the mountain is topped by telecommunications equipment the trail is well cleared and easy to follow, and hence requires only a few hours each way.

A little to the east and closer to the edge of the buffer zone, the tiny settlement of Lalawan, at an altitude of approximately 1,200 metres (3,940 feet), is a good starting point both for exploration of Mount Apolang and for a climb to the summit of Mount Dulang-Dulang. This trail passes through extensive farmland, before moving into forest on the steeper slopes, and the hike up and down requires at least one night on the mountain. The Lalawan area is used extensively by birdwatching parties as PEFI maintains a simple lodge here. A pair of Philippine Eagles nest near here, and sometimes it is possible to see them.

Opposite, top: *The mighty Philippine Eagle, the world's second largest raptor, is highly endangered but still found in the Mt Kitanglad Range.*

Above: *A large emergent forest tree near Lalawan, stands silhouetted against the dawn.*

SIARGAO ISLAND PROTECTED LANDSCAPES AND SEASCAPES

A Varied Archipelago

Lying off the northeastern tip of Mindanao, this protected area consists not just of the island of Siargao itself but also of a cluster of smaller islands and islets as well as much of the surrounding sea. Incorporating beaches, caves, mangroves, lowland rainforest and coral reefs, Siargao Island is recognized to be of major importance to Philippine conservation. As a result, it is one of the 10 priority protected areas that form part of the new Integrated Protected Areas System funded by the World Bank. Although parts of Siargao were protected as early as 1981, the entire area did not become a single protected area until 1996 when it was declared a Protected Landscapes and Seascapes site (a category covering regions in which the human population seems to be living in harmony with the environment and using its resources sustainably), covering an area of 157,375 hectares (388,880 acres).

The Islands of the Protected Area

At 67,725 hectares (167,350 acres), land makes up less than half of the park's total area, the remaining 89,650 hectares (221,530 acres) covering the reefs and fishing grounds of the surrounding seas. The largest landmass by far is Siargao Island itself, while to the south lie Bucas Grande, Bagum and Bancuyo Islands. There is also a host of small islands and islets, such as Daco, Anahawan and Mangantuc, almost all inhabited by at least one community of fishermen. Perhaps the smallest island of all is tiny Guyam, little more than a sand-bar bearing a few coconut palms, set in shallow seas and surrounded by seagrass beds and coral reefs, off the southeastern tip of Siargao.

The east and west coasts of Siargao are quite different. The former is exposed to the full force of the Pacific Ocean, and is characterized by a coastline that alternates between sandy beaches and rocky shorelines, with fringing coral reefs in some of the less exposed areas.

Map labels: Manila; Mindanao; Malaysia; Dinagat Sound; Sugbuhan Point; Santa Monica; Burgos; Dahican Island; San Benito; San Isidro; Halian Island; Mangancub Island; Casulian Island; Poneas Island; Del Carmen; Park Office; Pilar; Laonan Island; Tona Island; Siargao Island; Siargao Island Protected Landscapes and Seascapes; N; Cloud Nine; General Luna; Bucas Point; Dapa; Lahayay Island; San Miguel; Daco Island; Bagum Island; Bancuyo Island; Casulian Island; Bucas Grande Island; La Januza Island; Pamusaingan; Anahawan Island; Mam-on Island; Socorro; Suhoton Cave; Mangantoa Island; Hinituan Passage

Opposite above: *A quiet, sandy cove near Cloud Nine provides a convenient anchorage for local fishing boats, sheltered from the Pacific surf crashing on the distant reef.*

Opposite below: *Carefully punting a boat through waters too shallow to use the engine, towards tiny Guyam Islet.*

Above right: *A young fishing family sifts through its net for fish after a sweep through beachside shallows.*

Location: Off the northeastern tip of Mindanao, about 50 km (31 miles) from Surigao, the nearest mainland port.

Climate: There is no completely dry season, but the driest month is June. The heaviest rains are from November to January. Daytime temperatures range from 30°C (86°F) to 35°C (95°F), the hottest time being June. Humidity ranges from about 80% to 90%. These islands rarely, if ever, get hit by typhoons.

When to go: April through to September offer reasonable weather. July to October is the best time for surfers, as typhoons passing to the north whip up the surf here.

Access: Daily flights from Manila to Cebu, followed by high-speed ferry to Surigao in mainland Mindanao. From Surigao daily high-speed ferries run to Dapa, the largest town on Siargao. From other parts of Mindanao, express buses run frequently to Surigao, via Butuan.

Permits: Not needed.

Equipment: Walking shoes, swimsuits, sunblock, hat, camera, binoculars, and all diving and surfing equipment.

Facilities: Almost all accommodation is in General Luna and Cloud Nine. Boats can be hired at the Cloud Nine resorts or in General Luna, Del Carmen, Dapa and Socorro (Bucas Grande Island). Snorkelling equipment can be hired.

Watching wildlife: Coral reefs in shallow water, birds in the mangroves, monitor lizards in the forests and coconut groves.

Visitor activities: Boat riding, walking, snorkelling, surfing.

Right: *Cattle Egrets stand among mangroves near Del Carmen.*

Above: *A Collared King-fisher, a very common species, sits in a mangrove tree near Cloud Nine.*

Below: *A monitor lizard crawls through grass in a coconut grove.*

Beyond the outer islets, the sea shelves steeply towards the massive Philippine Trench, which reaches a depth of over 10,000 metres (38,000 feet) 80 km (50 miles) northeast of Siargao. The west coast is sheltered by Mindanao to the west, and so is shallow and calm. Here extensive mangroves, especially around the township of Del Carmen, cover an area of 8,600 hectares (21,400 acres), the largest mangrove swamp in Mindanao.

Inland, the landscape is a mixture of plains and low rolling hills, made up of coralline limestone, volcanic rock and alluvial soils. The highest point is just 283 metres (929 feet) above sea level. Agriculture and scrubland cover much of the inland area, plus a number of remnant lowland rainforests. The most extensive surviving forests are to be found on Bucas Grande Island, where there is also the Suhoton Cave, site of an underground river that is slowly becoming popular with visitors.

The population of the protected area is about 82,000, mostly concentrated into the townships of Dapa (the largest settlement), Del Carmen, General Luna, Pilar, San Isidro, Burgos and Santa Monica on Siargao itself. Livelihoods consist almost entirely of subsistence fishing and farming.

Fauna and Flora

Surviving old growth forests cover an area of 4,440 hectares (10,970 acres), while secondary forest takes up another 12,600 hectares (31,135 acres). Both contain dipterocarp trees, while the forests of Bucas Grande Island are also rich in the Ironwood tree, highly prized for its timber and which as a result is now very rare in the rest of the Philippines.

Siargao's fauna includes the Saltwater Crocodile, which lives in the vast mangrove swamp to the west of

Del Carmen. The Dugong and several species of marine turtle visit the more exposed eastern coasts, the latter nesting on some of the isolated beaches, the former feeding on the seagrass beds. On land, the list of animals includes the Philippine Tarsier, Malay Civet, monitor lizards, and at least 84 species of bird, including the endangered Philippine Cockatoo.

Exploring the Islands

Overseas visitors have been making their way to Siargao since the early 1990s, but not for the scenery or the sake of nature conservation. This is a newly discovered surf heaven: the Pacific swell that rolls into the islands' eastern shores sends up enormous waves that create some of the most spectacular surfing conditions anywhere in Southeast Asia. Surf breaks have been discovered up and down the whole of Siargao's east coast, but the most famous is on its southeastern tip, close to the town of General Luna and nicknamed Cloud Nine. Such is the magnetism of this name that it seems to have completely replaced this headland's original title, even among the locals, and any foreign visitor seen anywhere near Siargao is simply assumed to be heading for Cloud Nine.

For those more with scenery in mind, there is plenty of exploring to be done, much of it by boat. Some of the best beaches are around the smaller islands, such as Guyam (where there is also good snorkelling) and Daco, although there are also good beaches at General Luna in the southeast and at Burgos in the north. Pilar, on Siargao's east coast, has the magnificent Magpopongko Rock Formation. On Bucas Grande Island Suhoton Cave can be partially explored, while close by are the Magkahuyog Falls. It is also possible to hire a boat at Del Carmen for an exploration of the mangroves, while almost anywhere on Siargao Island it is possible to hire a motorbike to have a guided tour of the inland areas.

Unfortunately there is no dive operation on Siargao Island, although snorkelling equipment can be hired. Good snorkelling areas can be found by taking boat trips to the areas around Guyam and Daco Islands.

Above: *A mix of hard and soft corals form a healthy reef in the shallow waters off Guyam Islet.*

Above: *Fiddler crabs are a common sight in the mud of mangrove swamps.*

AGUSAN MARSH WILDLIFE SANCTUARY

A Vast Floating World

A vast freshwater swamp, holding an estimated 15 per cent of the country's entire freshwater resources, Agusan Marsh lies on Mindanao's eastern plain, surrounded by mountains and drained by the north-flowing Agusan River. Largely ignored by scientists and conservationists until the early 1990s, it has since been found to be home to a vast range of fauna and flora, some of it unique and endangered. As a result, it has been included as one of the country's 10 priority protected areas in the new Integrated Protected Areas System (IPAS).

An Enormous Sponge

The marsh lies at the confluence of several of the Agusan River's tributaries, draining the mountains of Davao and Agusan del Sur provinces to the south, the Bukidnon mountains to the west, and those of Surigao del Sur to the east and north. The result is that the marsh acts as a huge sponge, soaking up the excess water that pours down from the mountains, especially in the rainy season, creating a huge area for wetland wildlife and protecting the downstream towns and cities, especially Butuan, from the catastrophic floods that would otherwise occur. Most rain falls from October to March, and during this time water levels rise by four metres (13 feet) above their dry-season levels.

Opposite: *Agusan Marsh's unique swamp forest, the waters covered with purple-flowering Water Hyacinth.*

Above right: *Houses of the local Manobo people are built on rafts, tethered to trees or anchored to the marsh bed.*

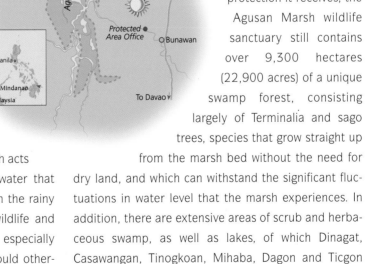

The entire marsh occupies over 72,000 hectares (178,000 acres), making it one of the largest freshwater marshes in the Philippines, although to date only 19,200 hectares (47,440 acres) have been included in the wildlife sanctuary, with a further 4360 hectares (10,775 acres) set aside as a buffer zone. The area consists of a great maze of interconnecting rivers, channels and lakes, with a few river banks and islands rising above the water, some permanently, others submerged during the rainy season.

Despite the incomplete protection it receives, the Agusan Marsh wildlife sanctuary still contains over 9,300 hectares (22,900 acres) of a unique swamp forest, consisting largely of Terminalia and sago trees, species that grow straight up from the marsh bed without the need for dry land, and which can withstand the significant fluctuations in water level that the marsh experiences. In addition, there are extensive areas of scrub and herbaceous swamp, as well as lakes, of which Dinagat, Casawangan, Tinogkoan, Mihaba, Dagon and Ticgon are the largest.

The Marsh's Wildlife

Agusan Marsh remained largely ignored until it was pointed out in the late 1980s that the Philippines' protected area system lacked freshwater marshes. When satellite photographs suggested that the marsh contained swamp forest it was decided to start some serious

Location: In Agusan del Sur province, northwest of the town of Bunawan, 150 km (93 miles) north of Davao, and 110 km (68 miles) south of Butuan.

Climate: Rain falls throughout much of the year, most heavily from October to March. Annual rainfall is 42.68 cm (168 inches). Daytime temperatures vary between 30°C (86°F) and 34°C (93°F), with humidity at 86%.

When to go: The period of least rain, in about July–August, offers the best weather, but falling water levels may make it difficult for boats to reach some of the lakes. Rainfall is very high during the peak of the rainy season, but high water levels make for a unique view of the marsh and allow access everywhere.

Access: Daily flights from Manila to Davao, followed by express bus (bound for Butuan) to Bunawan. Tricycle to the park office, and then boat hire for a tour of the marsh.

Permits: Not needed, but guidance from the park rangers will be needed.

Equipment: Rainproof clothing and bags, camera, binoculars, hat, insect repellent, anti-malarial prophylactics, food and water if intending to stay in the marsh overnight.

Facilities: Boats for hire in Bunawan and at the park office. Accommodation may be available near the park office.

Watching wildlife: Birdlife can readily be seen from a boat, particularly Purple Herons and egrets. Parrots and kingfishers are also commonly seen, as are some raptors, such as the Philippine Serpent-eagle.

Visitor activities: Boat riding, birdwatching, photography.

Right: *The trees of the swamp forest grow straight out of the marsh floor, without the need for dry ground, and are not harmed by changes in water level.*

Above: *A Purple Heron, a common bird in Agusan Marsh, takes flight.*

Above right: *Purple Swamphens lurk among the marsh vegetation.*

investigation. What was found was an enormous haven for wildlife, leading to the marsh's rapid inclusion on the priority protected list of the new IPAS.

In 1991 a survey found 262 species of wildlife, including 31 plant and 231 animal species. The latter contained 102 bird species, including Purple Heron and Oriental Darter, and 43 species of reptile, including large numbers of both Saltwater and Philippine Crocodiles, both highly endangered in the Philippines.

Most of this information was gathered in one relatively short survey that was not even able to penetrate into the remoter northwestern parts of the swamp. Since the vegetation of no Philippine swamp has yet been closely studied, it is very likely that many new species of flora, and perhaps fauna, await discovery here.

The Marsh People

Despite its isolation, the marsh is inhabited by about 2,600 people, more than half of whom consist of cultural minorities, mainly the Manobo, an animist group that live across much of eastern Mindanao. The remaining people are settlers who have moved in from other parts

Left: *Cattle Egrets fly low across the marsh.*

Above: *Locally caught fish, not surprisingly the staple diet of the marsh people, cut open and laid out to dry on the 'deck' of a floating house.*

Below: *A family of Manobo people, in their house, floating on the marsh's waters.*

of the Philippines. The marsh people live in floating houses, consisting of thatched timber or bamboo huts resting on a platform lashed to enormous logs. Whole communities exist like this, normally tethered in one spot although of course moveable at any time. During the dry season, the houses may still float on the lakes, or they may be allowed to land high and dry on some of the riverbanks and islands. The people live by growing a few crops, such as maize (corn), bananas and rice on the dry riverbanks and islands, as well as by fishing.

Exploring the Marsh

The marsh is most easily entered from the town of Bunawan, on the main road linking Davao and Butuan. Head for the park office a few kilometres northwest of Bunawan. Visitor facilities are still very limited, but it is intended to build accommodation here. The rangers will be able to offer advice on which parts of the marsh to explore, and may be able to help with the hiring of boat and guide.

Even from here, it takes about three hours to reach the marsh itself by boat. The riverbanks that earlier lined your route fall away, replaced by vast expanses of water, broken up into sections by walls of swamp forest growing straight out of the water, along with carpets of purple-flowering Water Hyacinth. One of the strangest sensations is that, when the boat's engine is switched off, you realise that the entire place is on the move. This is

not a motionless lake but a vast flowing river, ensuring that anything floating and not tethered will be carried relentlessly northwards towards the sea.

Manobo villages lie scattered in sheltered parts of the lakes or in narrow creeks, surprising collections of simple houseboats floating on the marsh. They are rather shy, humble people, but provided your guide is a native of the marsh you will be assured of a welcome at any of these villages.

MOUNT APO NATURAL PARK

The Philippines' Highest Mountain

At 2,954 metres (9,692 feet), Mount Apo is the Philippines' highest mountain, declared a national park in 1936. The mountain, an inactive volcano, lies west of Davao, in central-southern Mindanao, and covers an area of 72,110 hectares (178,190 acres), encompassing dense rainforests that spread across not just Mount Apo but also neighbouring Mount Talomo. The park is an invaluable refuge for wildlife, including the Philippine Eagle, and is one of the country's 10 priority protected areas. Several trails lead to the summit, and the climb is rapidly becoming one of the country's most popular hiking experiences.

A Mountain Landscape

The mountain rises up from the western shores of Davao Gulf, with relatively gentle slopes on the northern and southern sides, but very steep to the east and west. As a reminder that this volcano is not dead, there are a number of hot springs, the most accessible of which is Lake Agco, lying at an altitude of approximately 1,200 metres (3,900 feet) on the northwestern

Opposite: A gigantic Almaciga tree, the largest of the Philippines' forest trees, stands on the middle slopes of Mt Apo, shrouded in fog.

Above right: A wild balsam, or Impatiens, growing in the forest on the slopes of Mt Apo.

slopes. This small lake, surrounded by dense forest, is close to boiling point and continually pours off thick clouds of billowing steam. Nearby is a large new geothermal plant harnessing this energy, controversially carved out of the forest.

At about 2,400 metres (7,900 feet), nestled on a plateau, is Lake Venado – the remains of Apo's ancient crater, with the summit of Mount Apo lying to the southeast and that of Mount Talomo to the northeast. Apo has not erupted since 1640, but there is still some fumarolic activity just below its summit, with jets of steam and sulphurous smoke emitted from rocks on the steep eastern slopes.

The Mountain's Wildlife

Apo's uppermost 500 metres (1,600 feet) consist of rough and rocky grassland, but from Lake Venado downwards the mountain is covered with rainforest. Down to about 1,500 metres (4,900 feet) this consists of mossy forest, dense stands of gnarled trees with a canopy only 5-10 metres (16–33 feet) high, everything draped in thick layers of moss, ferns, orchids and other epiphytes. From 1,500 metres down to 1,000 metres (3,300 feet) is montane forest, consisting of taller trees, with a canopy about 20 metres (66 feet) high, with some much taller emergent trees. Below 1,000 metres grows lowland rainforest, consisting largely of dipterocarp trees, the giants of the tropical rainforest. Sadly, much of the

---

Location: Immediately west of Davao, straddling North Cotabato province to the west and Davao City to the east.

Climate: Rain falls quite evenly throughout the year, although April and May are drier. While daytime temperatures in Davao are 30–35°C (86–95°F), at Lake Agco they are 15–20°C (59–68°F), and around Lake Venado and the summit about 10°C (50°F) or much lower when raining.

When to go: The mountain can be climbed at any time of year, though April–May is likely to be the driest, sunniest time.

Access: Daily flights from Manila and Cebu to Davao. Express buses from northern Mindanao to Davao. Express bus from Davao to Kidapawan (2 hours), followed by jeepney to Lake Agco.

Permits: If climbing from Lake Agco, permits are obtainable from the Kidapawan Tourism Council.

Equipment: Take all your own camping equipment; hiking boots, food, warm and rainproof clothing and rucksack, leech socks, binoculars, camera.

Facilities: Accommodation in Davao and Kidapawan. Small lodge and campsite at Lake Agco. Philippine Eagle Nature Center at Malagos, near Davao. Guides and porters available at Lake Agco.

Watching wildlife: Around Lake Venado parrots can be seen, while Philippine Eagles, other raptors, hornbills and some mammals can be seen at the Philippine Eagle Nature Center. A number of wild birds can also be seen in the garden here, including the endemic Silvery Kingfisher.

Visitor Activities: Visiting the Philippine Eagle Nature Center, exploring around Lake Agco, birdwatching, hiking.

Right: *Philippine Eagles, although highly endangered, are scattered throughout the forests of Mindanao, including those on Mt Apo.*

lowland forest has been badly damaged owing to an ever-growing number of immigrant farmers.

The higher levels of forest remain in pristine condition, however, and in the montane zone there are stands of Almaciga, a Philippine endemic which, under the right conditons, grows to heights of 60 metres (200 feet), making it the country's biggest tree. Highly prized for both its timber and its resin, across the Philippines this tree has been heavily exploited and is now becoming rare. Here, on Mount Apo, although some have been lost, there are still extensive healthy stands.

Among the animal wildlife, 227 vertebrate species have been identified. Mammals include Philippine Deer, Philippine Warty Pig, Long-tailed Macaque, Philippine Flying Lemur and two species of civet cat. Small mammals include the Mindanao Tree Shrew, Mindanao Flying Squirrel and fruit bats such as the Golden-crowned Flying Fox; the world's largest.

Of the birds found on Mount Apo, 61 species are endemic to the Philippines, 14 of them restricted to Mindanao. The most famous of all is the Philippine Eagle, which is known to nest in and around the park. Over one metre (three feet) tall and with a wingspan of about two metres (six feet), this is the second largest raptor in the world, beaten only on weight by the Harpy Eagle of South America. A forest bird, its rapidly shrinking habitat has left the eagle endangered, with populations surviving only in remote areas of Mindanao, Samar and northern Luzon. Despite several studies, little is known about the bird, and estimates of the number surviving vary from 200 to 2,000.

Conservation Work

The Mount Apo area is well known for work by the Philippine Eagle Foundation, Inc. (PEFI) in attempting to ensure a safe future for this magnificent bird. Community work aimed at helping people living close to the forest to develop non-destructive livelihoods, coupled with efforts to recruit villagers living near known eagle nesting sites to protect the birds, have had some successes. A captive-breeding programme at Malagos near Mount Apo's eastern foot has been less successful, producing small numbers of chicks. Nevertheless the Philippine Eagle Nature Center has a valuable role in enabling both visitors and locals to get to know this bird at close range.

Climbing Mount Apo

Although there are several routes up the mountain, the most popular is from the west, starting at Lake Agco. To make this climb, first obtain a permit from the tourism

Right: *The Golden-crowned Flying Fox, one of the world's largest fruit bats, lives in Mt Apo's forests.*

Far right: *The Mindanao Writhed Hornbill has only recently been classified as a distinct species, endemic to Mindanao.*

office in the town of Kidapawan. Then take a jeepney to Lake Agco, where there are a campsite and small lodge, set in forest and close to the hot spring lake. Spend the first night here while guides and porters are organized.

From here, the first step is to pass through the gate to the geothermal plant, and then immediately leave the road and strike out up a track. This soon reaches a ridge, after which the path drops steeply down through forest to the Marbel River. You then follow the river upstream, frequently fording it as the valley becomes narrower and steeper, until a small plateau with a hot spring is reached. This is the last you will see of the river, for at this point the path starts the real climb, a very steep haul straight up the mountain through dense forests all the way to Lake Venado. The night's campsite is on the shore of the lake, with good views of the mountain summit.

Next morning, resume the hike before dawn in order to cover the two-hour climb either before sunrise or at least before the sun climbs high and clouds begin to gather over the mountain. Once at the summit, the view is stupendous, northwards across Lake Venado and the mossy forest towards Mount Talomo, and west down onto the geothermal plant and Lake Agco. This is as high as you can climb in the Philippines.

Above: *The summit of Mt Apo seen on a clear morning. It is important to reach the summit early in the morning, as on most days cloud and rain will arrive before lunchtime.*

Below: *Climbing Mt Apo involves numerous fordings of the Marbel River, not always an easy task.*

Top: *Lake Agco, surrounded by Mt Apo's forest, is a natural hot spring lake with a temperature close to boiling.*

Above: *After climbing Mt Apo, there is nothing quite as soothing as a soak in the hot spring bath adjacent to Lake Agco.*

Right: *The view from the summit of Mt Apo, across forest, Lake Venado and Mt Talomo.*

PALAWAN

Lying to the west of the main body of the Philippines, Palawan consists of one main island 425 kilometres (264 miles) long and 8–40 kilometres (5–25 miles) wide, associated with an estimated 1,768 smaller islands. It is oriented northeast to southwest, beginning with the Calamian Islands in the north and extending to Balabac Island in the south.

Palawan is often called the Philippines' 'final frontier', because it is still relatively under-populated and wild, with forests covering two-thirds of the land and extensive coral reefs teeming with life around its coasts. In 1990 UNESCO declared the entire province a Biosphere Reserve, an event that paved the way for a greatly expanded conservation programme.

The fauna and flora of Palawan are fundamentally different from those of the rest of the Philippines, the two being separated by the Wallace Line, which marks a division between Pacific and Australasian species to the east and Asiatic species to the west. Thus, Palawan's wildlife, unlike the rest of the Philippines, has many similarities with that of Borneo and mainland Southeast Asia. Here can be found such animals as Asian Short-clawed Otters, Bearcat and Mouse Deer, all animals not found in the rest of the Philippines, but widely scattered across Southeast Asia. There are, however, a number of animals utterly unique to Palawan, including 15 species of bird, perhaps the most famous of which are the Palawan Peacock-pheasant and the Palawan Hornbill.

Most visitors to Palawan come almost solely for its natural splendours. While getting around can be slow and difficult, the more adventurous are rewarded with some of the Philippines' most spectacular wild environments, from the incredible submarine world of Tubbataha Reef, to the unique St Paul's Underground River, and the stunning limestone cliffs of El Nido and Coron Island. For the downright odd, it is hard to beat Calauit Island, where herds of African mammals roam freely in this Philippine setting.

TUBBATAHA REEF NATIONAL MARINE PARK

The Heart of the Sulu Sea

One of the remotest locations in the Philippines, this reef lies at the heart of the Sulu Sea, approximately 160 kilometres (100 miles) southeast of Puerto Princesa, capital of Palawan. It is also the country's largest coral reef, covering 33,200 hectares (82,000 acres) and consisting of two atolls that rise up from very deep water to form two shallow lagoons and a number of islets. They are surrounded by some of the most spectacular sea life to be found anywhere in Southeast Asia, ranging from the tiniest corals to the biggest sharks and even whales. To protect this beautiful area the reef was declared a national marine park in 1988 and a World Heritage Site in 1993.

Previous pages:

Page 146: *Limestone rocks in the shallows close to Langen Island stand silhouetted against the dusk.*

Page 147: *The Clown Triggerfish, found along reef drop-offs, is readily identified by its large round white spots.*

Opposite far left above: *A Moorish Idol swims among brilliantly coloured soft tree corals.*

Opposite far left middle: *A Hawksbill turtle swims across hard corals.*

Opposite far left below: *A mixture of hard corals growing on the northern side of the north atoll.*

Opposite left: *A large sea fan, this huge coral is common on walls and steep drop-offs subject to strong currents.*

Above right: *A Brown Booby and its chick on Bird Islet.*

A Vast Reef Complex

The two atolls are aligned southwest–northeast, with the more northerly atoll the larger of the two, measuring approximately 16 kilometres (10 miles) long and 4.5 kilometres (2¾ miles) wide. It is separated from the smaller southern atoll by a channel eight kilometres (five miles) wide. Both atolls consist of very little land, mainly being vast shallow lagoons ringed by the reef flat and crest, parts of which are exposed at low tide. The reef crest marks the very edge of the atoll, for beyond here the submarine landscape plunges steeply into deep water.

The largest piece of land is Bird Islet, lying at the northern end of the north atoll. It is a small sandy island that rises barely two metres (six feet) above the sea, and is an important nesting and roosting ground for such oceanic birds as Brown Boobies and Brown Noddies. Another small islet, marked by a lighthouse, lies at the south end of the southern atoll, where terns, gulls and boobies can be found.

Each atoll is surrounded by a reef flat 200–500 metres (220–550 yards) wide, ending in a wall or steep drop-off into very deep water. The whole area teems with marine life, with the shallower parts rich in table and staghorn hard corals, the reef crest covered with a vast array of hard and soft corals, and the precipitous walls home to Gorgonian sea-fans, soft tree corals and *Tubastraea* cup corals. Fish life, estimated at nearly 400 species, includes just above everything imaginable from the tiniest reef fish through butterflyfish, Moorish Idols, trumpetfish, triggerfish, grouper, wrasse, sweetlips and

Location: In the Sulu Sea, approximately 160 km (100 miles) southeast of Puerto Princesa, with the north atoll at 8°50'N 120°00'E.

Climate: The reef is exposed to both southwest (June–October) and northeast (November–February) monsoons, so the seas are rough for much of this time. March to May is usually quite calm, with clear skies. Daytime air temperatures are then usually 32–35°C (90–95°F), while water temperature is 26–30°C (80–86°F).

When to go: March to May is the only time when the reef is accessible.

Access: By live-aboard dive boat operating out of Puerto Princesa in Palawan or Iloilo on Panay. Both can be reached by daily flights from Manila.

Permits: Your dive ship operator will take care of all this. To avoid disturbance to nesting birds visitors are not usually allowed to land on the islands.

Equipment: Some dive boats provide diving equipment, some do not. Check before departure and bring your own if necessary. Bring camera, hat, swimsuit, sunblock, reading material, sea sickness prophylactics.

Facilities: All accommodation aboard ship. All food provided. Divemasters know the reef well. Mooring buoys for dive boats.

Watching wildlife: Almost everything you could hope to meet in the sea! Several kinds of sharks, turtles, tuna, barracuda and a vast array of reef fish.

Visitor activities: Diving, photography.

Map labels:
Sulu Sea
Manila
Palawan
Malaysia
Bird Islet
Lagoon
North Atoll
Reef
Reef
Amos Rock
South East Sand Cay
South Rock
Tubbataha Reef National Marine Park
Black Rock
South Atoll
Lagoon
Reef
Lighthouse Islet
N

Above: *A Brown Noddy, resting in the trees on Bird Islet. The island is a major roosting and nesting site for oceanic birds.*

fishing industry, the larvae being carried westwards on the prevailing currents. The reef is thus not just a magnificent wildlife spectacle, but a vital component of the Philippines' coastal economy.

Conservation of the Reef

Situated far out in the Sulu Sea and surrounded by waters that are rather rough for nine months of the year, Tubbataha's own isolation has served as its greatest protector. However, since the mid-1980s an increasing number of fishermen have been fishing on the reef, at least some using dynamite and cyanide techniques. The resulting deterioration in Tubbataha's condition led to rapid moves to declare it a national marine park. Unfortunately, its isolation, as well as its vast size, have also made the reef difficult to police, and although some studies have shown it to be recovering it is still under pressure. Now managed by the Palawan Council for Sustainable Development (PCSD) and frequently patrolled by coastguard boats, it is to be hoped that the reef's protection will improve still further. The reef's 1993 inclusion in UNESCO's list of World Heritage Sites should increase its profile, conservation importance and hence protection still further.

batfish, to shoals of deep-sea fish including tuna, barracuda, fusiliers and jacks, as well as Whitetip, Blacktip and Grey Reef Sharks, Leopard Sharks, at least two species of dolphin and occasionally small whales. Manta rays, as well as Green and Hawksbill Turtles, are common.

It is believed that Tubbataha Reef produces most of the fish larvae needed to support much of Palawan's

Diving at Tubbataha

Despite some dynamite damage, this is still one of the most spectacular reefs in Souteast Asia. However, its isolation makes it difficult to reach, the only option being 4–5 day live-aboard cruises working out of either Puerto Princesa or Iloilo, and then only during the calm March–May period.

In order to minimize anchor damage, visiting dive boats must tie up at one of the limited number of

Above right: *Just a few centimetres long, the Squirrelfish is a ubiquitous resident of virtually every Philippine reef, and is especially common at Tubbataha.*

Right: *A Grey Reef-shark patrols the deep waters around the reef. Sharks are sighted during every Tubbataha dive.*

Above: *Bird Islet, part of the northern atoll, is almost circular and completely ringed with a dazzling white beach. The trees give good shelter to the many birds that use the island.*

mooring buoys provided, with divers then being ferried to nearby dive sites by launch. On each dive your launch will drop you at the reef crest, where your group will gather before plunging over the edge into a blue abyss. To one side is a vertical wall, covered with ledges, over-hangs and caves, as well as a wide variety of corals and sponges. On your other side is a vast blue nothingness from out of which may appear shoals of tuna or bar-racuda, as well as the occasional patrolling shark or groups of manta rays. There is no sediment suspended in this water, and visibility is usually well over 30 metres (100 feet). Reef fish are everywhere, a huge multi-coloured display of life, fluorescent greens and blues, orange or yellow spots or stripes; no attempt at camou-flage here, just a gaudy display. On the shallower parts of the dive hard corals spread across the reef flat, and along the sandy bottom turtles and Leopard Sharks are a common sight. Each and every dive is an exciting leap into a stunning undersea world, where something unusual is virtually guaranteed.

Left: *A group of Japanese divers comes in for a close look at Bird Islet, although landing is restricted in order to protect the colonies of breeding birds.*

Top: *At the end of a dive, air tanks are passed into the boat before the divers climb in.*

Above: *A Manta Ray, a common sight around Tubbataha Reef, glides gracefully past.*

Left: *Sunset over Bird Islet, the northernmost part of Tubbataha Reef, and site of a number of important bird colonies.*

St Paul's Underground River National Park

A Unique Flooded Cave Surrounded by Forest

Situated on Palawan's west coast 81 kilometres (50 miles) north of Puerto Princesa, the provincial capital, this well-protected national park, also known as St Paul's Subterranean National Park, is site of some interesting limestone rainforest, stunning coastal scenery and an underground river. The river runs for eight kilometres (five miles) through a limestone cave before flowing into a lagoon separated from the sea by a beach. It is surrounded by densely forested rugged limestone scenery, through which pass a number of trails that are worth exploring. Established in 1971 and today managed by the Palawan Council for Sustainable Development (PCSD), the park covers an area of 5,750 hectares (14,210 acres), along with a 290 hectare (720 acre) marine sector that protects the shoreline and offshore coral reefs.

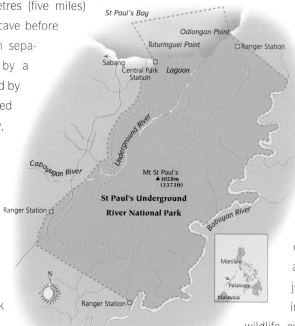

A Rugged Limestone Terrain

The area is surrounded by steep limestone hills and dominated by the 1,028 metre (3,373 feet) Mount St Paul's, which lies within the park's boundaries. The mountain obtained its name from British sailors aboard the HMS Royalist, which explored this coast in 1850. Apparently the mountain's dome-shaped outline reminded them of London's St Paul's Cathedral.

Today the park is high on the list of Palawan visitor attractions, although the place is much more than just a tourist site. Its dense forest is of immense importance to the area's wildlife, even though much of the land beyond the park's boundaries is also still forested. At the human level it is also the ancestral domain of one of the Philippines' smallest cultural minorities, the Batak tribe. Now numbering at most only 350 people, this group is in imminent danger of assimilation by the growing number of settlers in the area.

The source of the underground river is the Cabayugan River, one of several watercourses that drain the hills of the interior. The water filters through the porous limestone into caves within the mountains before forming a

Opposite above: The coastline of St Paul's Underground River National Park is a mixture of rocky foreshore and white beach, backed by dense forest.

Opposite below: The entrance to the Underground River is little more than a relatively small hole in a limestone cliff.

Above right: For those hiking into the park, a welcoming sign stands at the point where the path leaves the beach and enters dense rainforest.

Location: On the west coast of Palawan, 81 km (50 miles) north of Puerto Princesa and 4 km (2.5 miles) east of the coastal village of Sabang.

Climate: The rainy season lasts from late May or early June to September or October. The dry season is from November to May. Daytime temperatures are 30–35°C (86–95°F), coolest in January, hottest in May.

When to go: Go during the dry season, as the road to Sabang from Puerto Princesa is impassable in heavy rain. Best time is February to April.

Access: Daily flights from Manila to Puerto Princesa. From here, some hotels and tour operators offer daily tours to Sabang and the park, or alternatively Go Palawan, a travel agency, runs a daily minibus to Sabang. Public transport consists of very slow and unreliable jeepneys. From Sabang walk into the park or hire a boat at the Sabang wharf.

Permits: Obtain at either the national park office in Puerto Princesa or at the ranger station in Sabang.

Equipment: Walking shoes, torch (flashlight), insect repellent, antimalaria prophylactics, swimsuit.

Facilities: Accommodation in Puerto Princesa and Sabang; easily hired boats from Sabang to the park; well-laid trails in the forest; organized exploration of the underground river by boat.

Watching wildlife: Macaques, monitor lizards, Tabon Scrubfowl, insectivorous bats, swiftlets and forest birdlife.

Visitor activities: Birdwatching, swimming, cave exploration by boat, hiking.

dry soils that typically cover limestone areas. This is low-land evergreen rainforest, containing many dipterocarp trees, although here, owing to the thin soil, few reach the gigantic sizes normally associated with these trees. Animal life abounds, the most obvious being the large numbers of Long-tailed Macaques that live in the forest near the lagoon and beach. Two-metre (six-feet) long monitor lizards are also a common sight, often seen swimming across the lagoon. Other mammals include the Asian Short-clawed Otter, although it is most unusual for these shy animals to be seen. The park's caves are home to an uncountable number of insectivorous bats, which stream out in huge crowds at dusk in search of food. They share them with swiftlets, which fly during the daytime, returning to the caves at dusk, at pretty much the same time as the bats are leaving.

Other birdlife, concentrated in the forest, include Hill Mynahs, a bird valued in the pet trade for its ability to talk and which as a result is now locally endangered; the Tabon Scrubfowl, a chicken-like bird that scratches around in the leaf-litter and surface soil for food, and which is remarkable for the huge mound of soil that it builds over its incubating eggs; and the Asian Fairy Blue-bird, a gorgeous iridescent blue-and-black bird that is spread across much of Southeast Asia. The Palawan Pea-cock-pheasant, unique to this island, is also present in the forests of St Paul's, but being a shy, nervous bird the chances of finding one are very remote.

river that flows towards the sea through the eight kilo-metre (five mile) cave. The river finally sees the light of day, exiting through the cave's mouth, a six-metre (20-feet) high opening in a vertical and very jagged limestone cliff. The water flows into a lagoon separated from the sea by a sand-bar, but through which the water is able to flow to reach the sea.

Teeming with Wildlife

The lagoon is surrounded by dense rainforest, which stretches all the way from the beach right up into the fur-thest mountains, most of it adapted to life on the thin,

Cave and Forest Exploration

The park is reached from Puerto Princesa via the village of Sabang, located just a few kilometres west of the park and itself site of a spectacular and largely deserted

beach. From here one can enter the park either on foot or by boat. The former takes one along the beach and then, once inside the park, through dense forest on a well-made path all the way to the lagoon, a distance of about four kilometres (2 ½ miles). Alternatively, boats can be hired at Sabang's wharf, for a 15-minute journey into St Paul's Bay, where the boat drops you at a beach. From here, it is a 200-metre (220-yard) walk through forest to the lagoon.

On the shore of the lagoon rangers check permits and then arrange for outrigger boats to carry visitors into the cave, travelling one kilometre (½ mile) along the tunnel before turning around and returning. Each boat carries a powerful lamp, making it possible to see some of the stalactite and stalagmite formations, as well as the huge size of the cave through which the boats travel.

Outside, several well-marked trails allow for exploration of the forest without the need for a guide, two of the most popular routes being the Jungle and Monkey Trails. Macaques, monitor lizards and a range of forest birds are commonly seen. Tabon Scrubfowl are very common around the picnic area, just within the forest on the edge of the beach. Their huge nests can often be seen nearby.

Above: *Boats moored offshore at Sabang beach with Mt St Paul's behind.*

Below left: *A group of visitors explores the Underground River in a canoe.*

Below: *The Palawan Peacock Pheasant is a spectacular bird, but very hard to find in the forest.*

CORON ISLAND

Secluded Home of the Tagbanua

This rocky island to the southeast of Busuanga, main island in the Calamian group of islands and the northernmost part of Palawan, is only now in the process of becoming a protected area. One of the few parts of the Calamian Islands still to be forested, home both to rare wildlife and the rather shy Tagbanua people, one of Palawan's principal cultural minorities, this is a unique place. Only recently recognized for its importance in Philippine conservation, after some initial local opposition, the island and its surrounding waters are now becoming part of the Integrated Protected Areas System (IPAS), under the care of the European Union-funded National Integrated Protected Areas Programme (NIPAP), one of two large overseas-funded conservation programmes now operating in the Philippines.

Opposite above: *The beautiful inlet, surrounded by limestone cliffs, that forms the anchorage for boat parties heading to Kayangan Lake.*

Opposite below left: *A Tagbanua woman cleaning birds' nests. Trade in this material constitutes a valuable component of Coron Island's economy.*

Opposite below right: *A Tagbanua man mends his fishing net at the village of Cabugao.*

Above right: *A cashew nut, one of Coron Island's main crops, slowly ripens on its tree.*

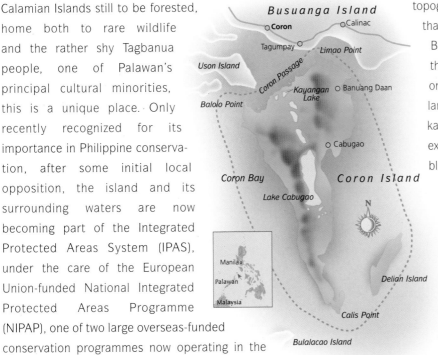

Karst Limestone Scenery

Shaped roughly as an elongated, inverted triangle, Coron Island forms the southeastern wall of enclosed Coron Bay, with the much larger Busuanga Island forming the bay's northern shore. Coron's topography is quite different from that of any nearby land. Whereas Busuanga's landscape, as well as that of other adjacent islands, is one of rolling hills, Coron consists largely of a mass of almost sheer karst limestone hills, making for an extremely rugged and impenetrable landscape.

The result is very beautiful. Many of the less vertical slopes are still densely forested, inhabited by a wide range of wildlife that includes rare tortoises, parrots, the Palawan Hornbill and 100–200 Philippine Cockatoos, a highly endangered endemic bird, whose total wild population throughout the Philippines has been estimated at between 1,000 and 4,000. Inland there are also seven lakes, typical of this type of limestone scenery, although most are extremely hard to reach.

The Tagbanua of Coron Island

The island is inhabited by about 1,000 Tagbanua, a rather shy and gentle people who live in two villages on the remoter eastern side of the island, facing the open sea. Here, at Banuang Daan, the more northerly of the two villages, and Cabugao, are two rare areas of flat land

Location: In the Calamian group of islands, the northernmost part of Palawan, to the southeast of Busuanga, largest of the Calamian Islands.

Climate: The rainy season lasts from late May or early June until October or November. The dry season is spread through the rest of the year, although there may be light rain in December and January. Daytime temperatures range from 28°C (82°F) in January to 36°C (97°F) in May. Humidity is always high, at 85–95%.

When to go: The best time is the cooler part of the dry season.

Access: There are daily flights from Manila to Busuanga, though only in clear weather. Jeepney from the airport to Coron town. From other parts of Palawan there are twice-weekly ferries from Taytay and Liminancong (near El Nido) to Coron town. In Coron town boats can be hired to reach the island.

Permits: Currently not needed for Kayangan Lake, but check with the protected area office in Coron town.

Equipment: Shoes to protect feet on sharp limestone rocks; swimsuit, hat, sunblock, anti-malaria prophylactics, camera, binoculars.

Facilities: Protected area office in Coron town; accommodation and dive operators in Coron town; boats for hire; footpath to Kayangan Lake.

Watching wildlife: Parrots, Palawan Hornbills, Philippine Cockatoos, other forest birds.

Visitor activities: Boat rides, birdwatching, swimming, snorkelling, diving.

Above: *Limestone forest trees, with many of their leaves shed during the dry season, an important protection against dehydration.*

that can be farmed. Much of these people's income is derived from fishing, although farming is also important, the main crops consisting of cashew nuts, banana, cassava, coconut and mango. Some of the permanent crops, including a number of new cashew groves, have been planted with the aid of overseas aid groups, including Conservation International, part of a growing band of alternative livelihood programmes designed to help rural people develop environmentally sustainable and non-destructive sources of income.

The island's limestone hills are riddled with caves that are home to millions of swiftlets, so Coron's Tagbanua also do quite well out of collecting their nests, a material that is so valuable as to be like gold dust to these villagers! The collecting season usually lasts from December or January until April, at which time collecting stops to allow the birds to lay eggs and rear young.

Generally speaking, the Tagbanua have a deep respect for their environment, and although now largely Christianized they still believe in spirits. They have

Right: *The fruiting body of a local herb, growing on the forest–farmland fringe.*

Far right: *The flower of the kapok tree, important as a source of stuffing for pillows and cushions. Kapok trees are common in the farmlands of Coron Island.*

worked to protect Coron Island's natural environment, revering the island's lakes as sacred and working hard to prevent outsiders moving in and causing damage.

Conservation Work

It is not simply chance and a rugged landscape that have protected Coron's forests, and it was this local concern for the environment that drew the attention of conservationists working in the early 1990s to create a new IPAS. However, the Tagbanua's own distrust of outsiders in general and government in particular made it very difficult for conservation plans to move forward. Progress finally came when the proposed management plan was translated by the local priest, an American who has lived on Coron for much of his life, from Filipino into the Tagbanua dialect. Since then, the local people seem to have embraced proposals to make Coron a protected area, allowing plans for control and protective measures to be implemented.

The entire protected area covers 7,580 hectares (18,730 acres), of which Coron makes up about half. The remainder covers the surrounding seas and a few outer islands, including Delian, an islet to the southeast that is occupied by immigrants from the Visayas. The main aim of protecting the seas is conservation of the coral reefs, most of which lie to the south and east of the island. The health of these reefs is paramount to the wellbeing of the Tagbanua's economy, yet there has been extensive dynamite damage caused by visiting outsiders, a problem the islanders have been powerless to prevent. It is hoped that the recent installation by NIPAP of a patrol boat will help bring destructive fishing methods here to an end.

Visiting the Island

The Tagbanua remain reluctant to accept outsiders, so much of Coron is off-limits to visitors. However, the one area that has been opened is Kayangan Lake, a beautiful spot on the northwest coast. A boat hired in Coron town, on Busuanga Island, will take you into a stunningly beautiful cove surrounded by towering limestone cliffs, to a point where you can disembark. A path leads over a short but steep pass and down into a valley where the lake lies blue and sparkling in the sunlight, again surrounded by sheer cliffs. It is possible to go swimming and snorkelling here. Dive operators in Coron organize diving trips to this lake. There is not a lot to see, but being fed by a hot spring, the temperature rises as you dive, reaching about 40°C (104°F) at a depth of 30 metres (100 feet).

Above: *An outrigger, tied up in the little natural harbour next to the village of Banuang Daan, with a huge limestone cliff towering above.*

Left: *A heavy liana climbs its way up a tree in the limestone lowland forest.*

CALAUIT ISLAND WILDLIFE SANCTUARY

A Piece of Africa in Asia

Lying in the remote north of the Calamian Islands, the northernmost part of Palawan, 3,750 hectare (9,265 acre) Calauit Island is a most unusual wildlife sanctuary. Established in 1976, it is home to six species of African mammals, which live here in almost completely wild conditions; offering a unique opportunity to see giraffes and zebras at home in an Asian landscape. The protection given to these mammals has also been good for the local Philippine wildlife, of course, and so the island abounds in Calamian Deer, a species almost extinct elsewhere, as well as a wide range of birdlife.

A Savannah Landscape

The island of Calauit is situated off the northern tip of Busuanga, the main island in the Calamian group, and is separated from it only by a dense and primeval mangrove swamp that covers an estimated 500 hectares (1,250 acres). Calauit itself has a landscape of low hills, a large proportion of which are covered in dense scrub. The island's seaward-facing coastline is a mixture of rocky shore and sandy beach, lined offshore by healthy and protected coral reefs that are included as part of the sanctuary.

Opposite: *A Calamian Deer surveys the scene on the savannah-like landscape of Calauit Island.*

Above right: *Some of Calauit's giraffes are sufficiently tame that they can be fed by hand.*

SOUTH CHINA SEA
Coral
Point Calauit
Manila
Palawan
Malaysia
Coral
Calauit Island
N
Coral
Park Headquarters
Boat Landing
Illultuk Bay
Mud
Coral
Mangrove
Quezon
Busuanga Island

Although fences prevent the animals from reaching some of the dense scrub areas, they are able to roam over much of the island, and in these parts it is astonishing how much they have affected the landscape. Here, the scrub has been largely cleared, leaving an open savannah-like environment, grasslands dotted with occasional clumps of trees and a few small scrubby bush areas.

African and Philippine Wildlife

It was in 1977 that the African mammals arrived, eight species brought in from Kenya as a conservation move at a time when it seemed as though much of that African country's wildlife was heading for extinction. Those eight species were giraffe, zebra, waterbuck, bushbuck, eland, gazelle, topi and impala, a total of 104 animals. The gazelle died out quite early on unfortunately, due to intense fighting among the males, and today the topi are struggling to hang on apparently because the zebras love to kick and bite the topi young! The other six species, however, are doing well, their numbers swollen to 550, with just three of the original imported animals still alive. The waterbuck and impala are doing especially well, with 160 and 182 animals respectively, although it is the giraffes and zebras that tend to be the most visible in the landscape.

The protection given to these African mammals has also been very valuable to the local Philippine wildlife.

Location: Off the northern tip of Busuanga Island, in the Calamian group of islands, the northernmost part of Palawan, at 12°20'N 119°55'E.

Climate: The rainy season lasts from late May or early June to October or November. Light rain falls during the dry season, from November to January, but then dry February–May. Daytime temperatures range from 28°C (82°F) to 36°C (97°F), the coolest month being January, the hottest May.

When to go: Go during the dry season, although April and May are very hot.

Access: Daily flights from Manila to Busuanga Island, then transfer to accommodation either in Coron town or on Dimakya Island. From Coron there is one daily bus to Quezon, the nearest village to Calauit, from where a boat can be hired. Alternatively, hire a boat in Coron for the entire trip.

Permits: Obtainable on landing on Calauit.

Equipment: Binoculars, camera, sunblock, insect repellent, antimalaria prophylactics, hat.

Facilities: Accommodation on Calauit is only for visiting staff and scientists. Accommodation is the luxury resort on Dimakya Island; otherwise one has to stay in Coron. On Calauit, rangers guide visitors on a truck.

Watching wildlife: Masses of wildlife. African mammals most likely to be seen are giraffe, zebra, eland, waterbuck and impala. Calamian Deer are easily seen. Captive crocodiles, Mouse Deer and Bearcat can also be visited. Birdlife is extensive, including pigeons, bee-eaters, drongoes and eagles.

Visitor activities: Bird- and mammal-watching, photography.

Above: *The fruits of a Sterculia species tree, a common sight on Calauit Island and a favourite of the giraffes.*

Above right: *Calauit Island's savannah-like landscape is characterized by occasional clusters of trees spread across the grasslands.*

When the project started the island was home to just 35 Calamian Deer, the largest surviving herd of this animal that, as its name suggests, is restricted to the Calamian Islands. Today, over 1,000 of the deer wander at will around the island, often seen in herds quietly grazing close to groups of giraffes. A number of deer have been moved to other unpopulated islands in the Calamian Islands, thus re-establishing herds in those places.

The island also abounds in birdlife, an estimated 120 species making use of the scrub' and savannah landscape. Many of the birds can be quite easily seen, including Green Imperial-pigeons, Black-naped Orioles, drongos and bee-eaters. Commonly seen raptors include the White-bellied Sea-eagle and Philippine Serpent-eagle.

A number of Philippine animals are also being captive-bred here, including the endangered Philippine

Crocodile, Palawan Bearcat and Mouse Deer, all housed in pens scattered around the sanctuary. In 1990 a typhoon destroyed part of the pen housing the Mouse Deer, allowing a number to escape. A recent survey found that these animals are now doing very well in Calauit's scrubby areas, a very encouraging sign since this nervous animal is virtually extinct in the Philippines, the only other site within the country where they survive being on Balabac Island in the far south of Palawan.

The island sanctuary is closely controlled by the Palawan Council for Sustainable Development (PCSD), a quasi-government body that manages most of Palawan's protected areas. An unfortunate part of setting up the sanctuary in 1976 was the forcible removal of all the island's inhabitants, an event that is now the focus of a legal battle as those people fight for the right to return. Tensions have been running high on the issue, creating some fear for the future of the sanctuary. Provided an agreement can be reached with the local people, the sanctuary should continue as a major site both for the conservation of native wildlife and, due to the rather incongruous presence of African mammals, as an attraction for Palawan's growing number of visitors.

Visiting and Touring the Sanctuary

Calauit offers a unique opportunity to mount an 'African safari' in the heart of Asia! Although it can be difficult to

A Philippine Crocodile at Calauit's captive breeding centre. Highly endangered, captive breeding may be the only way to save this species.

Left: *A herd of eland makes its way across open grassland. This is one of the species that has done very well since its introduction here.*

reach, once there a stunning experience awaits the visitor. The rangers guide visitors around by truck, stopping to view whatever herds of animals appear, and visiting the various captive-breeding pens. The zebras and giraffes are particularly approachable, the latter often agreeing to be fed by hand. The savannah landscape offers some great vistas, across grasslands and clumps of trees, with herds of eland moving across the 'African' scene, the occasional group of zebras here and there. On the most open grasslands, particularly near the park office, herds of Calamian Deer wander, at home here and yet strange companions to the African animals. Giraffes are often encountered, browsing on the scrub or some of the taller trees, while on a rare occasion it may be possible to see nervous bushbuck or the native wild pig lurking among the dense stands of bamboo.

Below: *A group of zebra standing in the dappled shade offered by a cluster of trees.*

EL NIDO MARINE RESERVE

A Magnificent Island-studded Bay

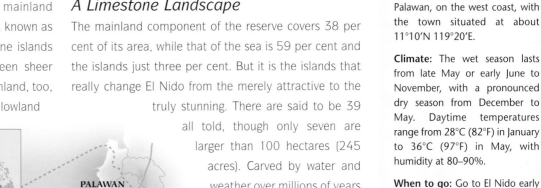

Lying close to the northern tip of mainland Palawan, El Nido consists of a wide bay, known as Bacuit Bay, studded with karst limestone islands that typically have small beaches set between sheer cliffs soaring vertically out of the sea. The mainland, too, has many such cliffs, and there are swathes of lowland evergreen rainforest covering an important watershed. Altogether, this is one of the Philippines' most beautiful locations, reason enough to protect it, although the main purpose in doing so is to safeguard the marine resources, in particular the turtles that nest on its beaches and the fish life that support the local human population. Small parts of the mainland's watershed forest have been protected since 1935, while protection of the bay's turtle areas started in 1984. It was only in 1991 that the reserve was expanded to take in the entire bay and mainland watershed forests, covering an area of 89,140 hectares (220,265 acres). It is now a part of the European Union-funded National Integrated Protected Areas Programme (NIPAP).

Opposite above: Huge limestone cliffs are typical of the islands of El Nido, as shown here at Langen Island.

Opposite below: Bacuit Bay's only township is called El Nido, a small settlement hemmed in by limestone cliffs.

Above right: The protected area office, on the main street in El Nido town.

A Limestone Landscape

The mainland component of the reserve covers 38 per cent of its area, while that of the sea is 59 per cent and the islands just three per cent. But it is the islands that really change El Nido from the merely attractive to the truly stunning. There are said to be 39 all told, though only seven are larger than 100 hectares (245 acres). Carved by water and weather over millions of years from even more ancient coral reefs, their towering rocky pinnacles are quite unknown in the rest of the Philippines. Indeed, the landscape has been likened to the inland karst landscape of southern China. This is not surprising, as it is believed that Palawan originated as part of southern China or northern Vietnam, before breaking away and drifting to its present location as part of the Philippines 17–40 million years ago.

Some of the islands are little more than jagged rocks protruding above the sea's surface, such as the three-peaked cluster of rocks known as Tres Marias. Others are large islands, forest-covered and dominated by one or more towering rocky peaks, such as Cadlao, Langen or Malapacao Islands. Others are known for their fearsomely jagged rocks and cliffs, covered only with very sparse and highly specialized vegetation. An example of this is Miniloc, a large island ringed with ferocious-looking cliffs and rocks, and well known for its two beautiful lagoons, hidden sea coves almost completely ringed-in by cliffs

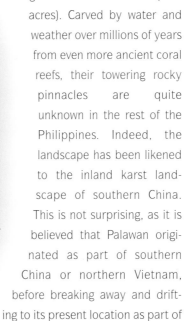

Location: In the far north of Palawan, on the west coast, with the town situated at about 11°10'N 119°20'E.

Climate: The wet season lasts from late May or early June to November, with a pronounced dry season from December to May. Daytime temperatures range from 28°C (82°F) in January to 36°C (97°F) in May, with humidity at 80–90%.

When to go: Go to El Nido early in the dry season, when there is no rain and temperatures and humidity are still comfortable.

Access: Daily flights from Manila direct to El Nido. Also daily flights from Manila to Puerto Princesa, followed by a combination of bus to Taytay (on Palawan's northeast coast) and then boat to El Nido. Twice-weekly ferries from Coron in the Calamian Islands to Taytay and Liminancong (near El Nido), followed by boat hire to El Nido.

Permits: Not needed, but the reserve's new management intends to introduce charges that will be incorporated into every visitor's lodging bill.

Equipment: Swimsuit, hat, camera, shoes for forest or limestone walking, sunblock, anti-malarial prophylactics. Diving and snorkelling gear can be hired.

Facilities: Accommodation in El Nido town and on islands; plenty of boats for hire; reserve office in El Nido town; beaches in town and on islands; nearby airport.

Watching wildlife: Marine turtles are common. On land the rare Palawan Hornbill, monitor lizards and Long-tailed Macaques can be seen.

Visitor activities: Boat riding, swimming, snorkelling, diving, birdwatching, walking.

Opposite top: *The shattered rocks of Tres Marias, one of the main emblems of El Nido.*

Opposite below: *The Miniloc Island Resort is one of the most exclusive places to stay in El Nido.*

Overleaf: *A sunset view of Cadlao Island, seen from El Nido town.*

Right: *Buttress roots help to support a large tree in lowland rainforest, on Langen Island.*

Below: *A Reef Egret does its fishing from a boat quay on Miniloc Island.*

In the north lies the area's only town, El Nido, a sleepy place consisting of just a couple of streets running parallel to one of the area's largest beaches, and itself hemmed in by high cliffs.

Fauna and Flora

El Nido's natural environment consists of a complete sequence of habitats from submarine coral reefs through seagrass and seaweed beds in shallow areas, mangrove or beach forests along the shores, to either lowland evergreen rainforest or limestone forest inland.

However, El Nido is far from being in pristine condition. Although its mainland hills are partially covered with lowland evergreen rainforest, logging from the 1970s until 1992 has left the forest cover rather patchy, resulting in unstable soils and unreliable water supplies. The forest is still quite healthy in places, however, with some of the best found on the larger islands.

Offshore, although there are spectacular corals in very shallow areas, in deeper waters most of the reefs have been badly damaged and fish stocks reduced to dangerously low levels. However, coral cover is significantly better than it was in the late 1980s, a sign that the measures put in place in 1984 to protect turtles is starting to work. Four species of marine turtle (Hawksbill, Green, Olive Ridley and Leatherback) are quite common, using the islands' hidden beaches for nesting, and the highly endangered Dugong is regularly seen in the bay, coming here to feed on the extensive seagrass beds. At least two species of dolphin (Bottlenose and Spinner) and two of whales (Bryde's and Humpback) frequent the area.

New controls on fishing and forestry, only now being implemented, should help to boost the reserve's natural environment in the coming years, allowing the reefs to recover and stabilizing the soils and water supply on land.

Tourism in El Nido

Despite its isolation, El Nido is rapidly becoming the latest 'hot' discovery, something of a tropical Shangri-la, with approximately 20,000 people arriving annually.

Although there are plans for some major developments, at present tourist facilities are relatively small and low-key, with simple resorts on several of the islands and the mainland south of El Nido town, plus a number of budget lodgings in the town itself.

Places that just have to be visited include Miniloc Island's two lagoons, where crystal-clear turquoise waters are surrounded by intensely green vegetation and sheer limestone cliffs, and where turtles are frequently seen. Many of the islands have isolated beaches, where a boat can drop you off, leaving you to play Robinson Crusoe for a few hours. Those that have dense rainforest can be explored provided there is a trail (such as on Langen Island, behind the new Ten Knots' Lagen Island Resort).

Beneath the waves, it has to be said that there is little for divers to get excited about, apart from probable encounters with turtles. However, some of the very shallow waters, such as around Tres Marias, have excellent coral cover and so are great for snorkelling.

SUMMARY OF CONSERVATION AREAS

The following is a brief summary of the protected areas known to be presently operational or in the process of being established. Most have been described in this book and are open to visitors. Visitor facilities are basic at most. Check with the 'Visitor Information' panels for each site, and for most contact the local protected area office before venturing in. Areas are rounded up.

Luzon

Bataan Natural Park (23,700 ha/58,500 acres). Province: Bataan. Proclaimed 1945. Rugged terrain of volcanic origin, covered with dipterocarp, montane and mossy forest. A priority protected area.

Batanes Protected Landscapes and Seascapes (Land: 23,000 ha/57,000 acres; Sea: 450,000 ha/1.1 million acres). Province: Batanes. Proclaimed 1994. Lowland rainforests, attractive coastline, coastal reefs and fisheries. A priority protected area.

Bulusan Volcano National Park (3,700 ha/9,100 acres). Province: Sorsogon. Proclaimed 1935. Active volcano with attractive lakes, grasslands, lowland and montane rainforest.

Hundred Islands National Recreation Area (1,850 ha/4,550 acres). Province: Pangasinan. Proclaimed 1966. Attractive collection of coralline limestone islands and rocks in Lingayen Gulf.

Mayon Volcano National Park (5,460 ha/13,490 acres). Province: Albay. Proclaimed 1938. The Philippines' most active volcano, having last erupted in March 2000. Towers above the city of Legaspi.

Mt Arayat National Recreation Area (3,700 ha/9,180 acres). Province: Pampanga. Proclaimed 1933. Inactive volcano rising up out of the central Luzon plains.

Mt Banahaw National Park (11,130 ha/27,510 acres). Provinces: Laguna and Quezon. Proclaimed 1941. A massive active volcano. Considered a sacred mountain, the area around the main hiking trail is deforested. Montane and mossy forests still survive in remoter regions.

Mt Data National Park (5,510 ha/13,620 acres). Province: Mountain. Proclaimed 1940. Remnant pine and mossy forests.

Mt Isarog National Park (10,100 ha/25,000 acres). Province: Camarines Sur. Proclaimed 1938. Inactive volcano with montane and mossy rainforest. Site of extensive biological research.

Mt Makiling Forest Reserve (4,200 ha/10,500 acres). Provinces: Laguna and Batangas. Proclaimed 1933. Inactive volcano with hot springs, covered with dipterocarp and montane rainforest. Important site for biological research, site of the Makiling Botanical Garden and Philippine Raptor Center.

Mt Pulag National Park (11,500 ha/28,400 acres). Provinces: Benguet, Nueva Vizcaya and Ifugao. Proclaimed 1987. Highest mountain in Luzon, with endemic wildlife, pine and mossy forests, and dwarf bamboo grasslands. One of eight sites in the National Integrated Protected Areas Programme.

Northern Sierra Madre Natural Park (360,000 ha/890,000 acres). Province: Isabela. Proclaimed 1997. Mountainous terrain, lowland rainforest, mangroves, beach forest, coral reefs, vast array of wildlife, including the Philippine Eagle. A priority protected area.

Quezon National Park (985 ha/2,430 acres). Province: Quezon. Proclaimed 1941. Lowland rainforest badly damaged by logging.

Subic Watershed Forest Reserve (10,000 ha/24,700 acres). Provinces: Bataan and Zambales. Proclaimed 1992. Lowland evergreen rainforest, mangroves, beach forest, extensive and easily seen wildlife, including important fruit bat colonies. Jointly with Bataan Natural Park, one of the country's 10 priority protected areas.

Taal Volcano National Park (4,540 ha/11,210 acres). Province: Batangas. Proclaimed 1967. A volcanic caldera lake containing an island on which sits one of the country's most active and dangerous volcanoes. Popular hiking area.

Mindoro

Apo Reef Marine Natural Park (15,800 ha/39,000 acres). Province: Occidental Mindoro. Proclaimed 1978. A sprawling atoll reef formation 30 km (19 miles) west of the Mindoro coast. Important as a fisheries resource and is a priority protected area.

Mt Calavite National Park (17,000 ha/42,000 acres). Province: Occidental Mindoro. Proclaimed 1920. Mountainous landscape, mostly grassland with some remnant forests. Important for its population of Tamaraw.

Mt Malasimbo Biosphere Reserve (Area unknown). Province: Oriental Mindoro. Proclaimed by UNESCO 1973. Mountain terrain with healthy forest and remnant montane and lowland forests.

Mts Iglit-Baco National Park (75,500 ha/186,500 acres). Provinces: Occidental and Oriental Mindoro. Proclaimed 1970. Rugged mountain landscape that includes Mindoro's second highest peak. A mixture of lowland, montane and mossy forests, along with grasslands. Home to the endemic Tamaraw. One of eight sites in the National Integrated Protected Areas Programme.

Naujan Lake National Park (21,650 ha/53,500 acres). Province: Oriental Mindoro. Proclaimed 1956. A large lake with volcanic origins, an important fisheries resource, and site for wading birds.

Puerto Galera Marine Reserve (Area unknown). Province: Oriental Mindoro. Proclaimed by UNESCO 1973. Spectacular and well-protected coral reefs, rich in barrel sponges and Gorgonian sea-fans.

Sablayan Watershed Forest (Area unknown). Province: Occidental Mindoro. Date of establishment unknown. Protected part of the Sablayan Penal Colony, consisting of a lake and lowland dipterocarp rainforest. Endemic birds, fruit bats, and said to contain a healthy population of Tamaraw.

Western and Central Visayas

Apo Island Protected Landscape and Seascape (Land 75 ha/185 acres; sea 284 ha/702 acres). Province: Negros Oriental. Proclaimed marine reserve in 1985, with entire island protected from 1995. A rocky island surrounded by excellent coral reefs.

Central Cebu National Park (6,900 ha/17,000 acres approx.). Province: Cebu. Proclaimed 1937. Once densely forested mountain range, now severely degraded. However, remaining forest fragments absolutely crucial as only homes to Cebu endemic birds, e.g. Cebu Flowerpecker.

Danjugan Island Marine Reserve and Wildlife Sanctuary (Land area: 75 ha/185 acres approx.). Province: Negros Occidental. Proclaimed 1999. A small island with rainforest and mangroves, surrounded by attractive coral reefs.

Mt Guiting Guiting Natural Park (15,700 ha/38,800 acres). Province: Romblon. Proclaimed 1996. The rugged dominant mountain of Sibuyan Island, rising up from sea level to 2,050 m (6,726 ft), covered in lowland, montane and mossy rainforest, and home to endemic wildlife. One of eight sites in the National Integrated Protected Areas Programme.

Mt Kanlaon Natural Park (24,600 ha/60,700 acres). Provinces: Negros Oriental and Negros Occidental. Proclaimed 1934. Active volcano and highest mountain in the Visayas. Lowland dipterocarp, montane and mossy rainforests. Endangered endemic wildlife, including the Visayan Spotted Deer and Visayan Warty Pig. One of the 10 priority protected areas.

Northern Negros Forest Reserve (86,600 ha/214,000 acres). Provinces: Negros Oriental and Negros Occidental. Proclaimed 1935. Mountainous terrain containing two inactive volcanoes. Lowland dipterocarp, montane and mossy rainforest, containing endangered endemic wildlife, such as the Visayan Spotted Deer and Visayan Tarictic Hornbill.

Olango Wildlife Sanctuary (920 ha/3950 acres). Province: Cebu. Proclaimed 1992 and became a Ramsar site in 1994. Mangroves and mudflats, essential to migratory birds.

Pescador Island Marine Reserve (Area unknown). Province: Cebu. Date of establishment unknown. Tip of a submarine mountain creating a small island, surrounded by pristine coral reefs and walls that plunge into deep water.

Southern Negros Forest Reserve (4,000 ha/10,000 acres). Province: Negros Oriental. Proclaimed 1967 (Twin Lakes area only). Inactive volcano with lakes plus lowland dipterocarp, montane and mossy rainforest.

Taklong Island Marine Reserve (1,150 ha/2,850 acres). Province: Guimaras. Proclaimed 1990. A small island off the southern tip of Guimaras, ringed by mangroves and coral reefs.

Eastern Visayas and Mindanao

Agusan Marsh Wildlife Sanctuary (19,200 ha/47,440 acres). Province: Agusan del Sur. Proclaimed 1998. A vast freshwater marsh, with swamp forest and extensive wildlife. One of 10 priority protected areas.

Balicasag Island Marine Reserve (Sea: 150 ha/360 acres). Province: Bohol. Proclaimed 1986. Coral reefs and steep drop-offs into deep water around a tiny, flat island.

Mt Apo Natural Park (72,110 ha/178,190 acres). Provinces: Davao City, Davao del Sur and North Cotabato. Proclaimed 1936. Inactive volcano and the Philippines' highest mountain. Cloaked in lowland dipterocarp, montane and mossy forests. Endemic wildlife, including the Philippine Eagle. One of 10 priority protected areas.

Mt Kitanglad Range Natural Park (30,650 ha/75,720 acres). Province: Bukidnon. Proclaimed 1990. Rugged mountain range, site of the Philippines' second highest mountain. Lowland dipterocarp, montane and mossy forests. Extensive birdlife, including the Philippine Eagle. One of 10 priority protected areas.

Mt Malindang National Park (53,260 ha/131,600 acres). Province: Misamis Occidental. Proclaimed 1971. Large mountain range with montane and mossy rainforest. One of eight National Integrated Protected Areas Programme sites.

Pamilacan Island Marine Reserve (Sea: 340 ha/840 acres). Province: Bohol. Proclaimed 1985. Scattered coral reef areas with nearby waters renowned for whales, dolphins, sharks and manta rays.

Rajah Sikatuna National Park (9,000 ha/22,300 acres). Province: Bohol. Proclaimed 1987. Hilly limestone landscape covered with forest. Large bird population.

Siargao Island Protected Landscapes and Seascapes (67,726 ha/167,351 acres). Province: Surigao del Norte. Proclaimed 1996. Remnant lowland rainforests, mangroves, attractive coastline, coral reefs, on the island of Siargao. One of 10 priority protected areas.

Sohoton National Park (840 ha/2,075 acres). Province: Western Samar. Proclaimed 1935. Limestone gorge, caves and natural bridge. Limestone forest.

Turtle Islands Wildlife Sanctuary (138,360 ha/341,880 acres). Province: Tawi-Tawi. Proclamation work initiated in 1995, but not yet complete. Six islands in the Sulu Sea, forming a transnational protected area with similar islands under Malaysian jurisdiction. Believed to be the only remaining nesting islands for Green Turtles in the ASEAN region. One of 10 priority protected areas.

Palawan

Calauit Island Wildlife Sanctuary (3,750 ha/9,265 acres). Province: Palawan. Proclaimed 1976. A unique savannah and scrub landscape occupied by African wildlife. Also numerous Philippine species, including the Calamian Deer.

Coron Island (7,580 ha/18,730 acres). Province: Palawan. Not yet fully established as a protected area. Karst limestone landscape with beautiful lakes. Dense forests with rare wildlife. Offshore coral reefs important to fisheries. Much of the island off-limits to visitors due to feelings of Tagbanua residents. One of eight sites within the National Integrated Protected Areas Programme.

El Nido Marine Reserve (89,140 ha/220,265 acres). Province: Palawan. Proclaimed 1991. Bay renowned for beautiful islands with limestone cliffs and beaches. Turtles common and some Dugong present. Lowland rainforest. One of eight sites within the National Integrated Protected Areas Programme.

Malampaya Sound (90,000 ha/222,000 acres approx). Province: Palawan. Not yet fully declared a protected area. A huge enclosed bay vital to fisheries, surrounded by well-forested land (lowland dipterocarp forest). Inner parts of the bay have some of the country's largest remaining undisturbed mangroves.

St Paul's Underground River National Park (5,750 ha/14,210 acres). Province: Palawan. Proclaimed 1971. A remarkable river flowing through a cave. Surrounded by dense lowland rainforest.

Tubbataha Reef National Marine Park (33,200 ha/82,000 acres). Province: Palawan. Proclaimed 1988. A vast atoll reef in the heart of the Sulu Sea. Great range of coral and fish wildlife, including turtles and sharks. Vital fisheries resource. A World Heritage Site.

Ursula Island Wildlife Sanctuary (10 ha/25 acres). Province: Palawan. Proclaimed 1960. A small island renowned for its birdlife.

USEFUL ADDRESSES

Department of Tourism
Rm 207, Department of Tourism Building, TM Kalaw St, Ermita, Manila
tel: 02-5242345; fax: 02-5218321

Haribon Foundation
3rd Floor, AM Building, 28 Quezon Avenue, Quezon City 1100, Metro Manila
tel: 02-7404989; fax: 02-7404988
E-mail: Haribon@phil.gn.apc.org

Kidapawan Tourism Council
Office of the Municipal Mayor, Kidapawan, Cotabato
tel/fax: 067-81604

National Integrated Protected Areas Programme (NIPAP)
Ninoy Aquino Park and Wildlife Nature Center, North Avenue, Diliman, PO Box 1614, QC-CPO, 1156 Quezon City, Metro Manila
tel: 02-9292034; fax: 02-9280805;
e-mail: asnipap@iconn.com.ph

Negros Forests and Ecological Foundation Inc (NFEFI)
South Capitol Road, Bacolod City 6100, Negros Occidental
tel/fax: 034-4339234.

NGOs for Integrated Protected Areas (NIPA) Inc
IPAS-PCU Office, Ninoy Aquino Park and Wildlife Nature Center, North Avenue, Diliman, Quezon City 1100, Metro Manila
tel: 02-9246031
e-mail: cppappcu@mnl.csi.com.ph

Palawan Council for Sustainable Development (PCSD)
3rd Floor, Capitol Building, Puerto Princesa City, Palawan
tel: 048-4332698

Philippine Eagle Foundation, Inc. (PEFI)
1 North St, DBP Village, Matina, Davao City
tel: 082-73360/2982063; fax: 082-2982757;
e-mail: Pheagle@dv.weblinq.com

Philippine Reef and Rainforest Conservation Foundation Inc (PRRCFI)
Door 3, Monfort Building, Mandalagan, Bacolod City 6100, Negros Occidental
tel: 034-7099262; fax: 034-4411658
e-mail: coralcay@mozcom.com

Protected Areas and Wildlife Bureau (PAWB)
Ninoy Aquino Park and Wildlife Nature Center, North Avenue, Diliman, Quezon City 1100, Metro Manila
tel: 02-9246031; fax: 02-9240109

Subic Bay Ecology Centre
Room 220, Building 255, Barryman Road, Subic Bay Freeport Zone 2222
tel: 047-2524435; fax: 047-2523891
e-mail: ecology@subic.com.ph

UNESCO National Commission of the Philippines
DFA Building, 2330 Roxas Boulevard, Pasay City, Metro Manila
tel: 02-8343447, 8344844

Whitetip Divers
Units 206/8/9, Joncor II Building, 1362 A. Mabini Street, Ermita, Manila
tel: 02-5268190; fax: 02-5221165
e-mail: whitetip@info.com.ph

World Wide Fund for Nature (WWF) Philippines
23-A Maalindog Street, UP Village, Diliman, Quezon City 1100, Metro Manila
tel: 02-4333220; fax: 02-9212912
e-mail: kkp@mozcom.com

FURTHER READING

Alcala, A.C. and Brown, W.C. (1998) *Philippine Amphibians: An Illustrated Field Guide*. Bookmark, Manila.

Allen, G.R. and Steene, R. (1994) *Indo-Pacific Coral Reef Field Guide*. Tropical Reef Research, Singapore.

Calumpong, H.P. and Menez, E.G. (1997) *Field Guide to the Common Mangroves, Seagrasses and Algae of the Philippines*. Bookmark, Manila.

Carcasson, R.H. (1977) *A Field Guide to the Reef Fishes of Tropical Australia and the Indo-Pacific Region*. Collins, London and Sydney.

Collar, N.J., Mallari, N.A.D. and Tabaranza, B.R. (1999) *Threatened Birds of the Philippines*. Bookmark, Manila (in association with the Haribon Foundation and BirdLife International).

Cusi, R. (1997) *The Philippine Coral Reefs in Water Color*. Jacoby Publishing House, Manila.

Davison, G.W.H and Chew, Y.F. (1996) *A Photographic Guide to the Birds of Borneo*. New Holland Publishers, London.

DuPont, J.E. (1971) *Philippine Birds*. Delaware Museum of Natural History, Greenville, Delaware.

Fisher, T. and Hicks, N. (2000) *A Photographic Guide to Birds of the Philippines*. New Holland Publishers, London.

Garcia, M.I. (1997) *Ecologica Filipina. The Almanac*. The Environmental Center of the Philippines Foundation Inc, Manila.

Gonzalez, J.C.T (1998) *A Pictorial Guide to Philippine Endemic Forest Birds of Mount Makiling, Luzon Island, Philippines*. University of the Philippines at Los Banos Museum of Natural History, Los Banos.

Gosliner, T. M., Behrens, D.W. and Williams, G.C. (1996) *Coral Reef Animals of the Indo-Pacific*. Sea Challengers, Monterey, California.

Heaney, L.R. and Regalado Jr., J.C. (1998) *Vanishing Treasures of the Philippine Rain Forest*. The Field Museum, Chicago.

Hicks, N. (1999) *This Is the Philippines*. New Holland Publishers, London.

Jackson, J. (1995) *The Dive Sites of the Philippines*. New Holland Publishers, London.

King, B., Woodcock, M. and Dickinson, E. (1975) *A Field Guide to the Birds of South-East Asia*. Collins, London.

Kuiter, R.H. and Debelius, H. (1997) *Southeast Asia Tropical Fish Guide*. Ikan-Unterwasserarchiv, Frankfurt.

Libosada Jr, C.M. (1998) *Ecotourism in the Philippines*. Bookmark, Manila.

MacKinnon, J. and Hicks, N. (1996) *A Photoguide to Birds of China, including Hong Kong*. New Holland Publishers, London.

Meyer de Schauensee, R.M. (1984) *The Birds of China*. Oxford University Press, Oxford.

Philippine Biodiversity. An Assessment and Action Plan (1997). Dept of Environment and Natural Resources, and the United Nations Environment Program, Manila.

Robson, C (2000) *A Field Guide to the Birds of South-east Asia*. New Holland Publishers, London.

Severino, H.G., ed. (1997) *The Green Guide. A Sourcebook on the Philippine Environment*. Philippine Center for Investigative Journalism, Manila.

Tan, J.M.L. (1995) *A Field Guide to Whales and Dolphins in the Philippines*. Bookmark, Manila.

Trono Jr, G.C. (1997) *Field Guide and Atlas of the Seaweed Resources of the Philippines*. Bookmark, Manila.

Viney, C., Phillipps K. and Lam, C.Y. (1994) *Birds of Hong Kong and South China*. Government Information Services, Hong Kong.

Wildlife Conservation Society of the Philippines (1997) *Philippine Red Data Book*. Bookmark, Manila.

Yin, R. (1997) *Beneath Philippine Seas*. Bookmark, Manila.

INDEX

ACKNOWLEDGEMENTS

The author/photographer would like to give sincere thanks to the following people and organizations, without whose help this book would have been impossible.

SPECIAL THANKS GO TO THE FOLLOWING ORGANIZATIONS
Makati Shangri-La Hotel, Manila; EDSA Shangri-La Hotel, Manila; Traders Hotel, Manila; Whitetip Divers, Manila; World Wide Fund for Nature, Philippines; Protected Areas & Wildlife Bureau of the Department of Environment & Natural Resources; NGOs for Integrated Protected Areas Inc; National Integrated Protected Areas Programme; Philippine Department of Tourism, London.
In addition, the following bodies and individuals were of great help:

IN THE PHILIPPINES
Manila Hotel, Manila; Hotel Sofitel Grand Boulevard, Manila; Shangri-La's Mactan Island Resort, Cebu; Bacolod Convention Plaza Hotel, Bacolod; Villa Margherita Hotel, Davao; Asiaworld Resort Hotel Palawan, Puerto Princesa; Sea Breeze Lodge, Coron; Fernando's Hotel, Sorsogon; Philippine Airlines; Philippine Convention & Visitors Corporation; Sorsogon Provincial Tourism Promotion Council; Department of Tourism, Legaspi and Davao offices; Kidapawan Tourism Council, Kidapawan; Whitetip Divers, Dumaguete; Savedra Dive Center, Moalboal; Genesis Divers, Alona Beach; Southern Cruise, Cebu; Philippine Reef & Rainforest Conservation Foundation Inc, Bacolod; Negros Forest and Ecological Foundation Inc, Bacolod; Philippine Eagle Foundation Inc; Haribon Foundation Inc; The Ecology Centre, Subic Bay Metropolitan Authority; Kitanglad Integrated NGOs, Cagayan de Oro; Center for Tropical Conservation Studies, Dumaguete.

IN THE UK
Fauna and Flora International, Cambridge; World Conservation Monitoring Centre, Cambridge; Bristol Zoo Gardens, Bristol; Rode Bird Gardens, Rode, Bath; Philippine Island Connections, London; Singapore Airlines, London; Coral Cay Conservation, London.

ELSEWHERE
Cathay Pacific Airlines, Hong Kong; Shangri-La Hotels & Resorts, Hong Kong; Singapore Zoological Gardens; Jurong Bird Park, Singapore.

FINALLY, A BIG THANK YOU TO THE FOLLOWING INDIVIDUALS
William Oliver; Sam Stier; Tammy Mildenstein; Caroline Manuel-Ubaldo; Neil Rumbaoa; Lourdes Tan-Arrieta; Joseph Arias; Gerry Ledesma; Juny Lizares; Lory Tan; Arnoud Steeman; Tony Wood; Sherry Villarin; Mary Claire Babista; Alda Valenzuela, Pamela Palma; Tony Sagun; Ely Alcala; JC Gonzalez; Andy Dans; Antonio de Dios; Ely Alcala; Duncan Bolton; Nigel Collar; Peter Raines; Joanne Watkins.

PHOTOGRPAHIC ACKNOWLEDGEMENTS
All the photographs in this book were taken by Nigel Hicks with the exception of the following:

Jack Jackson: p62 (bottom); p63 (bottom); p71 (top right); p75 (top) p105 (top right); p145 (top); p146 (right); p148 (centre); p151 (bottom right)

Lawson Wood: p14 (bottom right); p148 (bottom)

Left: *Palm fruits, Mt Malindang National Park, Mindanao.*